David Kadalie has placed his finger on the root cause for most of the ills plaguing the continent of Africa. Almost all of the problems facing African nations and the church can be attributed to leadership. As a student and practitioner of leadership, David draws from his vast and varied experiences in Africa to produce a masterpiece that any aspiring leader as well as those in leadership will do well to study, internalize and practice. Should you apply these principles, you will begin to see God transform your life, your ministry and your spheres of influence. This is a must read for every Christian leader.

> Don C. Osman
> Director of International Ministries
> Youth for Christ International

David Kadalie is a producer. He gets things done. Combine this drive with a spirit which longs to see leaders identified, trained & growing, & you have these 100 "Leadership Letters". And what David has written about, he has done.

Most of the Church's leadership development efforts have traditionally been focused on the already-developed world. These letters, written & rooted mostly in Madagascar, will serve to stimulate such growth in the under-developed world, especially in Africa. It has been said that the Church here is thousands of kilometres broad but only two centimetres deep.

May this compilation serve to deepen the Church in Africa through deepening its present & future leaders.

> Geoff Rutter
> Former Chairman,
> Youth for Christ South Africa

David Kadalie has taken over 25 year's experience in Youth Ministry and Leadership Training and Development and has made that available to aspiring and established leaders in this book. It covers in a very practical manner a very wide variety of aspects of leadership relevant in the Church, public and personal domains. This is a rich resource for anyone who is seeking to understand leadership and who also wants to be shown how it is done. Anyone who wants to know what it means to lead and how to lead will benefit from this book. I heartily recommend it.

> Dr. Charles Dickson,
> CEO St Dunstan's Association.

youth for christ botswana
Raserura Ward, Mochudi
P.O. Box 2574, Gaborone
Tel/Fax: (+267) 5728640

This is indeed a masterful, systematic, and carefully structured teaching on leadership and people development. David not only makes a strong case for the centrality of leadership in Christian organisation but also clearly lays out principles that are inspirational and thought-stimulating for any leader in pastoral calling. I can boldly say that the book is a provocative material, its themes and theses are passionately presented by an outstanding and experienced African leader of influence with the passion for effective church leadership in this century.

K. THOMAS RESANE
Senior Pastor,
Assembly of God Kempton Park

Leadership is broad, it's nebulous, it's about a lot of things - the Leader, Vision, Character, Skills, and Followers. But reading and knowledge are a fraction of the value. Growth only happens through actual changes in what you believe, how you think, how you react, what you prioritize, what you say, and what you do each day .. A book is simply entertainment unless you let the many truths of God's Words seep deeply into your soul transforming you to the full person who God designed you to become. Are you on that journey? Are you ready to wrestle through the application of leadership truths to the life you are living ~ before God, at the office, in your church, with your family, before strangers? If so, this book will take you through a process of reflecting and growing that will be unparalleled. Grab a pen and keep it close. I am already praying for your development and what God is planning to do with the bigger, stronger, deeper, happier, more effective, better you!

Sherlyn W. Farrell, CPA
President and Founder
Seven Kites Strategic Consulting, Inc. USA

DAVID KADALIE

Leader's Resource Kit

Tools & Techniques
to develop your Leadership

© Copyright 2006

Publisher: Evangel Publishing House, Nairobi, Kenya

ISBN 9966-850-94-5

First Printing 2006

Design & Layout Consultants: Ascent Creative, Nairobi, Kenya

Contributing Editor: Kirk Kauffeldt, Pan Africa Christian College, Nairobi, Kenya.

Printing by: Print House India Private Limited

Contents

Preface

As a pioneer for Christ for many years, my passion has been to develop young leaders. For me, there is nothing more fulfilling or rewarding than seeing a young person become a follower of Christ and then be discipled and developed into a godly leader who can impact the eternity of many others.

Perhaps this was first instilled in me by a pastor friend who mentored me and provided me with the tools to do what I love doing today ... he always stressed the importance of discipling and investing in others. These reflections, written while I was serving in Madagascar, are an indication of this passion.

Beyond my own passion for leadership development, I am joined by Youth for Christ International in Africa which shares a strategic focus on this integral characteristic. Our continent has been brought to its knees because of corrupt, unjust and dictatorial leaders. Raising a new generation of young godly and morally upright leaders has become our highest priority. We need to help them develop character and the skills necessary to rise to the challenge of influencing culture at every level ~ family, church, work and government.

My initial commitment to exploring leadership was a personal exercise to evaluate my own leadership, expose my blind spots, and identify where I could enhance my effectiveness. In the next step of development, I had opportunity to regularly share this passion with our supporters and other YFC leaders in Africa. And, as is so often true with God, He has had other plans for these thoughts on Leadership that I couldn't even begin to anticipate. With His divine orchestration,

I continue to be encouraged by hearing that these letters have become a blessing to many around the world who I didn't even imagine having an opportunity to touch!

I humbly and lovingly dedicate these reflections to our young YFC Malagasy leaders in Antsirabe who work week-by-week with these principles and whose interaction and feedback has been so valuable and integral in the development of this material. I would also like to thank so many other "leadership thinkers" out there who have encouraged and challenged me. And I must note how much I cherish the love, encouragement, prayers, and support of so many from around the world.

A special note of thanks...

To Sherrie Farrel for taking the initiative to convert the initial writings into a user friendly book format, and in so doing, providing me with a kick-start to get the book published.

To Wilbur van Niekerk for the many hours spent in the strategic positioning of the book, and assisting with designing the Reflection Questions and the Index.

To Geoff Rutter for being a mentor and friend over many years, for taking time, for the initial edit and for providing constructive input during the process of writing the book.

To Eshter Nyaga and Josleen Soita of Nairobi, Kenya for their hard work of getting the reference details in place.

But all of this would be hollow and empty without noting the immense gratitude I feel toward my lovely wife Denise. She has been alongside of me as a parent to our wonderful sons, as a minister for Christ to the lost and growing, and through my own spiritual development ~ hers have been the first eyes to see and enhance these concepts as they have been written one by one these past several years.

So with that introduction, I pray that God uses this book to touch you in a mighty way for His Kingdom. I would so value hearing your personal stories of the impact of leaders and leadership development and invite your comments to dkadalie@telkomsa.net.

Blessings on you!

David Kadalie

Editorial Comment

Good leaders develop and mentor other leaders. This task requires a number of prerequisite commitments. First there is commitment to personal growth and development as a leader. This begins with education, training and experience. Continual learning through reading, research and listening to others must follow these foundational activities. A second prerequisite is the commitment to share what you as a leader have learnt with others. To do this well, the leader must identify topics that are relevant and timely and then share them with those they are leading in a way that encourages and builds the capacity to lead. Finally, and perhaps most importantly, the leader must model what they are sharing with credibility and integrity.

David Kadalie is such a leader. Over the course of his service in YFC International, David cared for, served and led a number of staff members. By all reports he did this quite well. One of the practices that David invested his time in was the regular communication of leadership development materials through letters to his team members. Whether sparked by events or circumstances at the time, or the opportunity to share something practical that he had just come across, David would faithfully write lessons on leadership to his team members. His commitment to personal growth is evident in the number of authors or speakers he engaged in one way or another. A quick review of the collection of his letters illustrates the wide exposure he encountered. This exposure, however, was not just for his benefit and he faithfully shared with others what he had read and why he thought it was helpful material for leaders. His writing demonstrates that this sharing was done in a credible manner. In this fashion, he developed leaders.

David's letters have been collected, categorized and edited for the sake of a broader audience. They are many summaries of leadership lessons learnt from many different people – some well known and some undiscovered. David collected and distributed this wisdom over time and shared it with those he was providing leadership to. This resource kit is a summary of what he has learned from many others now assembled in an effort to improve and assist the task of leading.

Part I

UNDERSTANDING LEADERSHIP

The term 'leadership' is a difficult term to define. For every leadership theory, and there are a lot out there, there is a unique understanding of what the term describes. While achieving consensus about the definition of leadership may be impossible, leadership is an important part of our human experience that we all relate to. As such we have an intuitive sense of what leadership is all about. Most people can distinguish between a good leader and a bad leader without having done any study on leadership. However, for those who are leaders it is unacceptable to simply exercise one's leadership out of the intuitive sense one has about leadership. Leaders ought to examine their leadership and become increasingly intentional about doing whatever needs to be done to become a good leader, or an effective leader. For the Christian leader the evaluation of one's leadership must be critically informed by the revealed truth of God's word. This section of reflections provides opportunity to consider the essence of leadership.

1 Leadership Defined

I am discovering more and more that there is confusion about the term 'leader'. On the African continent some are clueless when it comes to leadership and even an embarrassment to say the least. Leaders are needed in every sphere of life and our challenge is to understand leadership, especially Christian leadership.

Leadership has been defined differently by many authorities on the subject. In fact, there are hundreds of definitions with many more emerging each month. Warren Bennis rightly says, "Without question, leadership is the most studied and least understood topic of any I can think of". There are three definitions I think are worth considering. The first one is by Field Marshall Montgomery;

> I. "Leadership is the capacity and will to rally men and women to a common purpose, and the character which inspires confidence."

In this definition we see the difference between "being" and "doing". We see three factors in giving leadership, followers, the act of leading, and the character of a leader:

- There must be followers. Do you have willing followers?

- The words 'capacity', 'will', 'rally' and 'common purpose' each describe aspects of what leaders do. There must also be clear direction. Where are you taking your followers? Do they own the vision?

- The phrase 'character that inspires confidence' highlight what a leader needs to be. There must be evidence of an exemplary character. Do we serve and model values?

Another good description of leadership is by Dr. J. Robert Clinton

> 2. "Leadership is a dynamic process in which a man or a woman with God-given capacity influences a specific group of God's people toward His purposes for the group."

In this definition we see four profound leadership truths:

- In leadership there is a dynamic process - you cannot lead every group or individual the same way

- In leadership there is a giftedness - *This is a God-given capacity*

- In leadership there is a major role - *it is a platform from which we influence*

- In leadership there is a goal - *to make people aware of their sense of God given destiny*

A third leadership description I would like to consider is one by Garry Wills.

3. "Leadership is mobilising others toward a goal shared by the leader and followers".

There are four key attributes in this definition which I would like to briefly highlight by considering the leadership of Christ with His disciples.

- A leader mobilises people. *Jesus mobilized his disciples. We see this in the feeding of the five thousand (Matt 14:13-21); as the disciples were sent out two by two (Luke 10:1-12); In the Great Commission when he said 'go ye into all the world'. (Matt 28:19)*

- A leader is focused. *Jesus demonstrated his clear commitment to do the will of His Father. Similarly Jesus commissioned them "to make disciples of all nations." As the Father has sent me, so send I you.*

- A leader works 'with' people. *Jesus shared his life and calling with His disciples. They operated as a team.*

- A leader has willing followers. *Jesus invited those he called to choose to follow him. The disciples were very committed to Jesus and, as it turns out, even willing to die for Him.*

Reflection

1. What would have to change in your character for you to inspire people towards a worthwhile purpose?

2. How would you incorporate your new understanding of leadership in your life?

3. What would you have to do to be remembered as the kind of leader you aspire to be?

2 The Leadership Challenge

As a leader I am continually learning the importance of challenging people. This involves urging individuals to reach their full potential and not settle for anything less than God's best. There are too many folks out there who do not believe in themselves. In view of this, I am learning to regularly give words of encouragement or make helpful suggestions. Sometimes I give a direct challenge or ask challenging questions. There are so many opportunities staring us in the face and needs that we must address. We must prompt others we can influence to take action.

A friend of Charles Colson gave him a simple challenge, to read "Mere Christianity" by C.S Lewis. That challenge changed his life and today he is a respected Christian leader of this century, an author of many books and the founder of Prison Fellowship Ministries, one of the largest evangelistic prison outreaches in the world.

Let me challenge you today with regards to leadership . The leadership challenge is probably one of the greatest facing us today. In our leadership we will face immense difficulties that may seem insurmountable, but this is what leadership is all about.

As leaders we need to take up the following...

o The challenge to be value driven

o The challenge to lead in a world that has turned into a global village

o The challenge to build a client-centred organisation

o The challenge to respond innovatively to accelerated change

o The challenge of leveraging technology

o The challenge to think strategically

The challenge to become a learning organisation…and so on

Our individual responses to many of these challenges differ

1. Some are over-cautious with millions of reasons why not to do anything.

2. Some are gripped by fear and go into some form of paralysis.

3. Some find every excuse in the book to run away from the challenges.

4. Some will quickly suggest another's name to avoid taking personal risk and responsibility.

5. Some just choose to ignore the realities and challenges of today and find immense comfort in the status quo.

6. Some moan, complain and make constant negative remarks, unaware of the incredible challenges staring them in the face.

7. Some, without much thought, get excited and grab these challenges with both hands.

8. Some prayerfully take a step of faith and respond in obedience to the challenges they face.

In the midst of all of this dynamic activity associated with leadership it is important to remember the essential functions of leading. By appropriately giving priority to the essentials we will exercise leadership that is grounded in principles. According to Dr. J. Robert Clinton the following are some of the leadership responsibilities. These are the 'challenges' to an aspiring Christian leader.

1. To develop and equip other leaders

2. To develop leaders for a multitude of tasks

3. To develop emerging leaders

4. To develop leaders to their full potential

5. To develop leaders with strong Biblical values

6. To develop leaders who embrace the challenges of today

7. To develop leaders with a good ministry philosophy

8. To develop leaders who operate within their gifting and natural abilities

9. To develop leaders who are taking responsibility for their own personal development

10. To develop leaders who have direction and purpose

11. To develop leaders who are committed to grow and finish the race well

Reflection

1. What prevents you from taking up leadership challenges?

2. What do you understand to be your leadership challenges, and how do you plan to proactively pursue them?

3 The Difference between Leadership and Management

In the late seventies and early eighties I was confused, as I read books on the topics of leadership and management. It seemed that the terms 'leadership' and 'management' were used interchangeably. I have also observed that confusion regarding the meaning and functions of leadership and management has created a great deal of misunderstanding, both in classrooms and in the workplace. In today's leadership literature this has generated considerable attention and there is an important clarification between the terms. In order to amplify this let me say emphatically that Leadership is not Management. The functions of leadership differ greatly from those of management. Each has its own characteristics and meaning, yet they are complementary. Both are desperately needed in our fast developing and complex societies. The word **manager** has as its root the Latin word *'manus'*, meaning 'hand'. From that root, it branches etymologically into the old French word *manege*, which means training and directing horses in a riding school. The word **leader** comes from the Anglo-Saxon word *laed*, meaning *'path' or 'road'*. The verb *laeden* means 'to travel'. The origin suggests a more distant, long-term orientation than does merely teaching a horse how to behave.

A number of scholars have developed helpful definitions and descriptions of the two concepts 'Manager' and 'Leader' including the following:

- George McGregor Burns, a political scientist and one of the first to delve deeply into the issue.
- Abraham Zaleznik wrote an article in the Harvard Business Review on the subject.
- Warren Bennis, a leadership scholar did a great job in distinguishing the leader and the manager in his book, *On Becoming a Leader.*
- One of my favourite leadership scholars Manfred Kets De Vries also has a great article in his book *The Leadership Mystique.*

Lets distinguish the two

The manager does things right (efficient);	The leader does the right things (effective).
The manager administers (control the affairs of a business);	The leader innovates (introduce new things).
The manager focuses on systems (orderly way of doing, arranging things) and structures;	The leader focuses on people (relationships must work).
The manager relies on control (regulate affairs);	The leader inspires trust and knows how to empower his or her followers.
The manager has a short-range view (focus on the present);	The leader has a long-range perspective (interested in the future).
The manager prefers stability (making sure business is firmly established);	The leader is interested in change.
The manager is preoccupied with rules and regulations;	The leader is caught up with vision (far-sighted, entrepreneur, adventuresome etc).
The manager is consensus driven (collective agreement and opinion);	The leader has the courage of his/her own conviction.
The manager is motivated by questions of procedure (a regular way of doing things);	The leader is more concerned about issues of substance (the essential part of the business).
The manager asks how and when;	The leader asks what and why.
The manager enjoys complexity (things that are difficult to understand);	The leader knows how to simplify.
The manager has his eye on the bottom line (the crucial factor or essential point);	The leader has his eye on the horizon (what is about to happen or that which is apparent).
The manager relies on logic (ability to reason correctly);	The leader uses intuition (understanding or feeling things immediately without conscious reasoning).
The manager accepts the status quo (state of affairs as it is now);	The leader challenges it.
The manager follows orders;	The leader initiates.
The manager is preoccupied by corporate concerns;	The leader has a wide outlook that encompasses social concerns.

The relationship between leadership and management is not an 'either or' matter. Every leader must have some management capacity and every manager ought to have some leadership capacity. Both are required, so the question is one of priority or emphasis. The common trap is for leaders to fall into patterns of management and abdicate their leadership responsibilities. The Bible is full of both leadership and management principles, which should be applied today. There are also examples of biblical leaders who serve as role models in this area.

The leadership of Nehemiah can be easily described as a manual on 'how to lead and manage'. Nehemiah demonstrated both functions. Geoff Rutter calls him the 'Effective Executive' and Charles Swindoll, in his book, 'Hand me another brick' says that the book of Nehemiah is 'a manual for leaders'.

As a manager

- **He knew how to organize a project** 3:1-32. He enlisted all classes of people for different tasks. Here he applies management skills.

- **He was goal orientated and focused** 5:16; 6:3. He could not be sidetracked from his major objective of rebuilding the walls. He was single-minded 4:6

- **He invested much time in thinking and planning ahead**. Facts before decisions.

- **He knew how to delegate responsibilities.** He handled the work in manageable tasks and assigned responsibilities. He was definitely not a 'one-man show' but knew how to delegate and collaborate with others to get the job done.

- **He gave incentives**

- **He knew the value of teamwork and synergy** 2:7-18; 12:31; 3:1-4:6.

As a leader

- **He was concerned about the events of the day** 1:1-3. He showed care for the plight of his people and asked questions about the destruction of Jerusalem.

- **He demonstrated a Godly character** 1:4-2:12. His first response to the crisis was to go into a time of mourning, fasting and prayer for his people. He confessed the sins of the people, showed concern about their lack of response to the Scriptures, and knew how to listen to God. He allowed a time of solitude for God to give him clear direction.

- **He was a man of balance** 2:4-6; 4:9. He exercised faith in God but also realised his personal responsibility to make plans. He exemplified sacrificial service for a cause servant leadership (2:5). He was prepared to give up a fine position because a greater work had to be done.

- **He was a man that was proactive** 2:11; 7:1-4. He waited on no one. Once he got the vision, he evaluated and took the initiative to mobilise the forces to rebuild the walls.

- **He was a motivator of people** 2:3; 2:17-18; 3:28; 4:14. He used courtesy, good preparation, incentives and appealed to the deepest needs of others to move them to action.

- **He handled conflicts** 5:1-19. He dealt with discouragement within his ranks by getting them unified, focused and mobilised.

- **He handled opposition** 6:1-19. He prayed and showed persistence when faced with the threat of violence, ridicule, the spreading of rumours, intimidation and criticism.

- **He was a man of integrity** 5:10, 14-19. He was against any form of extortion and believed in clean dealings. He refused to exploit the privileges he had.

- **He was a man of courage** 7:64, 13:8. He was willing to make tough decisions.

- **He had a giving spirit** 5:10. He denied himself the right to interest.

- **He was a man who promoted purity** 13:15. He has proven his purity and now demands purity in others.

- **He was a man who had a weakness** 13:5, 15, and 25. He did not seem to have trained or appointed a successor. In his 12-year absence you see a definite deterioration in all that he had accomplished.

Peter Daniels, an Australian friend of Youth for Christ, says in one of his books,

> "Managers have followers while they are in office; Leaders have followers even when they are not in office".

The challenge to all of us is to move away from the notion that if you are a good leader then there is no need to be a good manager and if you are a good manager then there is no need to be a good leader. You cannot separate the two functions. Both are needed. If you are a strong visionary leader and not a manager, decide today to develop those skills or find an assistant with management skills to complement your ministry or business. Some are high on leadership and low on management and some high on management but low in leadership. Leaders need to have their vision implemented and managers can only do their work well if they know in which direction to go.

Reflection

1. Which skills are lacking within you, and what will you do to make sure they are adequately fulfilled?

2. Have you identified whether you are more of a Leader or a Manager?

3. What will it take for you to become competent as a Leader and as a Manager?

4   Ten Things Leadership is NOT

Sometimes the best way to understand what something is, is to be clear about what something is not. There are many wrong perceptions of leadership, For example, my ministry with Youth for Christ took me into many schools. Often I saw the person with the highest academic qualifications become the principal of a school, even though they possessed no leadership experience or ability. Likewise churches choose great preachers to be leaders of God's flock. I must confess that I fell into that trap. I made someone with the biggest mouth a leader. What I got was more 'lip' but little leadership.

1.   Leadership is not management

In our previous reflection we looked at this more closely. Management is essentially the stewardship of resources, and its concern is for making the organisation more efficient. It involves itself with logistics, information and systems.

2.   Leadership is not administration

Administration is seeing that everything functions as it should. We know that work must be done conscientiously. It is necessary for the paper work to be done adequately…but this not leadership.

3.   Leadership is not ministry

Ministry is the effective exercising of the gifts God has given a person. This may make the person the best preacher or the best Bible teacher or the best counsellor but not the best leader. Managers manage, administrators administer, ministers minister - and leaders lead.

4.   Leadership is not titles or position

Titles, position and a big desk do not make a leader. It is more than "an office", whether appointed or elected. Seeking dominance and status is part of our corrupt nature. Matt 20:25-28. Matt 23: 5-12. Luke 11:43.

5.   Leadership is not degrees

MA, Ph.D., etc behind a person's name only proves that he or she is well educated. But that does not make them a leader.

6. Leadership is not personality

Too often organisations and churches are ruled by "personalities" who are not qualified leaders. They are outgoing and most often extremely self-centred. They may fill leadership positions but their motives are impure. Mark 12:38-39.

7. Leadership is not WHO you know or WHAT you know

It is who you are."Asking who is the leader is like asking who sings the tenor part in a quartet", said Henry Ford. To be the leader does not mean that you are more superior, or more gifted, or more intelligent, or more valuable than anyone else. Roman 12:8. It merely means that you are differently gifted and that you have a different role.

8. Leadership is not just genetic

Leaders are born and made. There are knowledge and skills of leadership that must be learnt - by observation, by experience, by systematic training and by on-the-job mentoring.

9. Leadership is not doing things TO people or FOR people

Doing things TO people often leads to exploitation. Ex 18:14

Doing things FOR people usually leads to paternalism.

Leadership get things done through and with people. Ex 18:21-22. Luke 9:1-6 and 10:1-20.

10. Leadership is not a science but an art

Maths, science, engineering are exact sciences. Leadership is an art. Just as each artist expresses himself or herself differently, so each leader expresses themselves in their own unique way.

Reflection

1. Are there other wrong perceptions of leadership that you could include in this list

2. How would you go about your exercise of Leadership based on your understanding on what it is not?

5   What is Really Expected of Leaders

At a recent Youth for Christ General Assembly in Brazil, I eaves-dropped on a conversation between two people. They were con-cerned that someone was being set up to fail as a leader. Some of us do appoint leaders for all kind of reasons. But leaders must be expected to lead, allowed to lead and empowered to do so effec-tively. We cannot appoint people in this position without giving them the role, authority, resources and training to do the job. Leadership is a function, not a title or position. It is something you do. Ted Carr, a former National Director of Youth for Christ South Africa and present CEO of ProVision International made a simple yet very profound statement, "For any serious enterprise to succeed, leadership is essential".

So, if you choose leaders they should have the ability and be expected to do the following:

They must set direction

To develop, articulate and share a vivid vision of a desired future that is challenging, credible, meaningful and worthy of pursuit. They create images of what could be and build excitement, instill-ing confidence, offering criteria for success and get people mov-ing. This also means creating a group identity and helping them to connect, dream together and trigger the collective imagination.

They must be change agents

To have an innovative urge to make the vision achievable in a changing environment. This would include research, training, human resource development and the empowering of people to act. Risk taking and flexibility would be essential characteristics.

They must be communicators

The ability to portray the vision clearly and in a way which enlists the support of followers. The leader is a skilled communicator and concerned listener.

They must be decision makers

To have the authority to establish strategies to facilitate change needed to achieve the vision. Get data and information, grab opportunities, study trends, seek expert opinions; do research to make the right choices.

They must align people

To create coalitions of committed people who understand the vision and who are committed to its achievements. People with administrative, managerial, fundraising, financial, creative, legal, accounting and ministry abilities.

They must motivate and inspire

To keep people focused and moving in the right direction, facilitating, encouraging, talking and living the vision, overcoming objections and obstacles, appealing to values, emotions and what could be.

They must be mentors

To be team builders who equip and empower individuals in the organisation. To adopt a style of coaching to help them understand the ethos of the organisation, themselves and the team they work with. To help them understand the importance of constructive feedback and the celebration of achievements. To make them feel respected, trusted and loved.

They must be role models

To live out in practice what they advocate with the mouth. Their lives must be considered as a standard of excellence to be imitated. What they are says more than what they do. What they do says more than what they teach. Their lives entail both "doing" and "being". To demonstrate servant leadership.

"If a man's gift is leadership, let him govern diligently" (Romans 12:8)

Reflection

1. Identify the leaders around you and rate them according to their effectiveness in doing the things on the list.

2. Which of these do you struggle with in your own leadership, and what will you have to do to overcome them?

6 Leadership as a Calling

Quite often the issue of 'call' comes up in conversations about leadership. In Christian ministry this cannot be ignored. I have learnt that the most 'qualified' leader can bring much disappointment if there is no clear sense of call.

John R.W Stott describes this kind of person well. "Many young men are looking for a safe job in which they can feather their nest, secure their future, insure their lives, reduce all risks, and retire on a fat pension. There is nothing wrong in providing for your future, but this spirit pervades our lives until life becomes soft and padded and all adventure is gone. We are so thickly wrapped in cotton wool that we can neither feel the pain of the world nor hear the Word of God... Jesus did not remain in the social immunity of heaven, or hide away in the safety of the skies. He entered the zone of danger; risking contamination..."

For those in leadership it is imperative to be motivated by a deep and a real sense of call. This is the heart of ministry; sensing God's call and direction and the joy of discovering how God uses you to fulfil His purpose. One's sense of call will define their leadership experience.

Too often we find people who are content:

- With doing the bare minimum but who demand maximum benefit
- With mediocrity and being under-achievers
- To be thrown around by the wind with no aim and purpose in life
- To be self-centred and largely motivated by status and prestige
- With their own security and who couldn't care less about the needs of those around them

The Scripture portrays many leaders motivated by a clear sense of call

1. Paul - "For Christ's love compels us..." 2 Cor.5:14. We see godly motivation

2. Moses - "By faith Moses when he had grown up, refused to be known as the son of Pharaoh's daughter..." Hebrews 1:24. We see a denial of royal privilege

3. Abraham - "By faith Abraham, when called...obeyed and went, even though he did not know where he was going" Hebrews 11:8. We see total obedience and willingness to risk with God

4. Jesus - "I have brought you glory on earth by completing the work you gave me to do" John 17:4. We see a single-minded focus and commitment

Many Christian leaders over the ages have also demonstrated their calling. David Brainerd, an early missionary to the Indians of the USA was so consumed with a sense of call that he claimed,"I cared not how or where I lived, or what hardship I endured, so that I could gain souls for Christ".The founder of the Salvation Army, William Booth remarked, "As far as I know, God has had all there was of me".Dawson Trotman of the Navigators saw the difference between a mere believer and a labourer. He made the statement that, "God can do more with one man that is 100 per cent dedicated to Him than with 100 men that are 90 per cent."

If your leadership is just a job with no sense of call then the following will be true:

1. You will be more concerned about your rights than God's rights to your life

2. You will be more concerned about the benefits than the mission

3. You will be more concerned about success than obedience

4. You will be more concerned about being a boss than a servant

5. You will be more concerned about your own future than that of others

6. You will be more concerned about external security than internal security

7. You will be more concerned about being a people pleaser than being accountable to God

Reflection

1. In your opinion, are you a leader by calling, by default, by appointment, by position, or by choice?

2. What can you point to in your leadership that demonstrates your sense of calling as a leader?

7 Jesus Christ the Greatest Leader who Ever Lived

I am so appreciative of my parents for introducing me to the greatest leader that ever lived, Jesus Christ. At the tender age of eight I made a commitment to be His follower. Most of my years have been dedicated to serving Him and there is no better description than this of our Lord:

"He never wrote a book. He never held an office. He never had a family or owned a house. He didn't go to college. He never visited a big city. He never travelled two hundred miles from the place where he was born. He did none of the things one usually associates with greatness.

He had no credentials but himself. He was only 33 when the tide of public opinion turned against Him. His friends ran away. He was turned over to His enemies and went through a mockery of a trial. He was nailed to a cross between two thieves. While He was dying, His executioners gambled for His clothing, the only property He had on earth. When He was dead, He was laid in a borrowed grave through the pity of a friend. Nineteen centuries have come and gone and today He is the central figure of the human race and the leader of mankind's progress.

All the armies that ever marched, all the navies that ever sailed, all the parliaments that ever sat, all the kings that ever reigned, put together, have not affected the lives of men on this earth as much as this man - Jesus Christ.

Today, two thousand years after His death, He is still alive, changing lives and bringing new meaning and hope. Only through Him can true happiness, peace with God and eternal life be found."

- Author unknown

There are several ways that Jesus exemplified characteristics of a true leader

He was visionary

He had a clear view of His destination, which made Him proactive rather than reactive. He could see the fields ripe unto harvest (John 4:35). He could see the good news of the Kingdom being preached in the whole world as a testimony to all nations (Matt 24:14). He could see an end time when all His followers would be gathered in, receiving their inheritance prepared for them in the Kingdom (Matt 24:34).

He was able to persevere

He resolutely set out for Jerusalem when the time drew near for Him to die. Luke 9:51. He endured till the end, till all was accomplished, till He could proclaim, "It is finished". John 19:30

He was a man of prayer

He persisted in prayer, sometimes throughout the night. He only made decisions when real communication was established. John 8:28

He was anointed

At the start of His ministry the Holy Spirit came upon Him in the form of a dove. Thereafter the Gospels constantly talk of Him living an anointed life. Luke 4:1,14,17; Acts 1:2

He exercised humility and grace

Matt 20:20-28 states it perfectly. Jesus washed feet and told his disciples to do the same. John 13:1-17. He lived sacrificially towards His followers - always going the extra mile, praying for them, blessing them, forgiving and nurturing them.

He was a team-builder

He built a team around Himself, which He was able to send into the world to preach the good news to all creation. Mark 16:15. He could tell them, "As the father sent me, I am sending you". John 20:21. He was a loving friend with a servant's heart. He was vulnerable and transparent and kept no secrets. He was a self-initiator with definite goals, which He communicated clearly. He knew hard work and knew how to confront. He recognised and rewarded team efforts.

Reflection

1. Which of these characteristics will you apply in your life and how?

2. What will you have to change in you in order to adopt Christ-like leadership attributes?

3. What can you do today to increase your influence where you are planted now?

8   Godly Leadership Qualities

I have a passion for developing leaders. Much of my time is spent in training others…but the New Testament book of I Timothy has challenged me no end about the qualifications of true spiritual leadership. Those of us who serve in this capacity must be so qualified that people will willingly follow our leadership.

When discussing leadership with his protégé Timothy, the Apostle Paul uses a couple of important terms: elder, bishop and deacon or deaconess. The term 'elder' likely refers to spiritual maturity and the responsibilities associated with this standing. The term 'bishop' involves the responsibility of oversight. The office of 'deacon' or 'deaconess' was created to solve organisational problems associated with the rapid growth in the church. I want to suggest that all Christian leaders are to demonstrate traits of maturity, give oversight to their followers and must have some organisational ability.

The following leadership qualities are noted in 1 Timothy. They provide a comprehensive checklist of aspiring Christian leaders to reflect on:

Desirable personal qualities and characteristics

- Leadership aspirations - 1 Tim 3:1. A decision not treated lightly in the early church

- Blameless character - I Tim 3:2. Strive to have a life that is above reproach

- Sensible judgement - I Tim 3:2. Keeping your head in all situations

- Self-controlled- I Tim 3:2. Do not cheapen ministry by foolish behaviour

- Well behaved - 1 Tim 3:2. Means orderly and decent in appearance and conduct

- Willingness to work - 1 Tim 3:13. Will lead to greater opportunities for ministry

- Not lover of money - 1 Tim 3:3. Content whether you have much or little

- Not violent - 1 Tim 3:3. Learn to disagree without being disagreeable

- Not quarrelsome - 1 Tim3: 3. Don't go about looking for a fight.

- Not a drunkard - 1 Tim 3:8. Abstinence not demanded but watch testimony

- Not double-tongued - 1 Tim3: 8. You can depend on their word. Yes is yes, no is no

- Not pursuing dishonest gain - 1 Tim 3:8. Watch out for deals that erode character

- Not a tale-bearer - 1 Tim 3:11. Watch gossip and slanderous talk

Social qualifications

1. A person with one spouse - 1 Tim 3:2. Polygamy and promiscuity prohibited

2. A good manager of the home - 1 Tim 2-4. If not, then you're a disqualified minister

3. A person with a godly family 1 Tim 3:4,5. Responsible behaviour of spouse and kids

4. A hospitable spirit - 1 Tim 3:2. Literally, loving the stranger

5. A good reputation - 1 Tim 3:7. A good testimony with those with whom you do business

Spiritual qualifications

1. Gentle - 1 Tim 3:3. Being thoughtful and patient in your dealings with others

2. Not a novice - 1 Tim3: 6. Give time for study and spiritual growth

3. Worthy of respect 1 Tim 3:8 A Christian character worth imitating

4. Doctrinally sound - 1 Tim 3:9. Must know and live the Word of God

5. Tested and credible - 1 Tim 3:10. Could do more harm than good if not proved

6. Able to teach - 1 Tim 3:2. Be a careful student of the Word of God

Reflection

1. If somebody joined your team or organisation today, which of these characteristics would you want them to be able to point to in your leadership?

2. How would you go about adopting some of these godly leadership qualities in your life and work?

9   A study on Leadership Traits in the Life of Nehemiah

I love the bible story of Nehemiah and have read this Old Testament book many times. There are many leadership principles that can be mined from this rich book. Every Christian leader should make a personal study of this book. Geoff Rutter calls Nehemiah, 'The effective executive'. Charles R Swindoll, in his book, 'Hand me another brick', says that the book of Nehemiah is 'a manual for leaders'. I am amazed at how relevant the principles are in this twenty-first century.

Consider the following leadership principles that can be learned form the life of Nehemiah:

1.   He was concerned about the events of the day 1:1-3

He showed care for the plight of his people and asked questions about the destruction of Jerusalem.

2.   He demonstrated total dependence on God 1:4-11

His first response to the crisis was by going into a time of mourning, fasting and prayer for his people.

3.   He identified with his people 1:6

He confessed sins together with the people.

4.   He was a man of the Scriptures 1:8

He was concerned about the lack of response to the Word of God

5.   He knew how to listen to God 2:12

He allowed time of solitude for God to give him clear direction.

6.   He was a man of balance 2:4-6; 4:9

He exercised faith in God but also realised his personal responsibility to make plans.

7.   He exemplified sacrificial service for a cause 2:5

He was prepared to give up a fine position because a greater work had to be done.

8. He was a man that was proactive 2:11; 7:1-4

He waited on no one. Once he got the vision, he evaluated and took the initiative to mobilise the forces to rebuild the walls.

9. He was a team person 2:7-18; 12:31; 3:1-4:6

He was definitely not a 'one-man show' but knew how to delegate and collaborate with others to get the job done.

10. He was a motivator of people 2:3; 2:17-18; 3:28; 4:14

He used courtesy, good preparation, incentives and appealed to the deepest needs of others to move them to action.

11. He knew how to organize a project 3:1-32

He enlisted all classes of people for different tasks. As a leader he also had management skills.

12. How to handle conflicts 5:1-19

He dealt with discouragement within his ranks by getting them unified, focused and mobilised.

13. He could handle opposition 6:1-19

He knew to have and showed persistence when faced with threats of violence, ridicule, the spreading of rumours, intimidation and criticism.

13. He was single-minded 4:6

He could not be sidetracked from his major objective of rebuilding the walls.

14. He was a man of integrity 5:10, 14-19

He was against any form of extortion and believed in clean dealings. He refused to exploit the privileges he had.

15. He was a man of courage 7:64 13:8

He was willing to make tough decisions.

16. He had a giving spirit 5:10

He denied himself the right to interest.

17. He was a man who promoted purity 13:15

He had proven his purity and demanded purity in others.

18. He was a man who had a weakness 13:5, 15, and 25

In his 12 year absence you see a definite deterioration in all that he had accomplished. He did not seem to have trained or appointed a successor.

Reflection

1. Rate yourself on a scale of 1 to 10 in each of the 18 traits mentioned above.

2. Identify the trait which is the strongest and which is the weakest?

10 How Leaders Relate

Leaders are normally expected to do many different things, but one thing that is for sure, leaders must know how to relate to others. This involves, discovering how God made people and knowing how to interact with and treat them accordingly.

This is an area I have had to work hard at. I'm still learning and will continue as long as different people come my way.

The heart of any organisation or church is the people in it and these people have to be understood, cared for, trained, developed and mobilized if they are going to make a significant contribution in the Kingdom of God. We cannot escape the fact that we are in daily contact with people. Leaders are visible and exposed to others whether they like it or not. There are management and administration demands, which we cannot ignore. Regular meetings and public engagements are expected but if we are going to lead then we better learn how to relate. We must understand that a good leader achieves his or her objectives through relationships.

The following concepts provide counsel on how we as leaders ought to relate to people.

1. Our priority is to disciple others. The whole process of discipling is patterned on the process of parenting (1Thess 2:7-12). Paul tells the Thessalonians in verse 11, "We talked to you as a father to his own children - don't you remember? Pleading with you and even demanding that your daily lives should not embarrass God..." Leaders ought to be like loving fathers taking their young followers under their wing, nurturing them until they are strong and mature to stand on their own.

2. Our development of others should be approached from a long-term relationship basis. John Maxwell has a development model, which consists of five progressive components.

    · I model it - I do it.

    · I mentor - I do it and you watch me.

    · I monitor - You do it and I watch you.

    · I motivate - You do it.

    · We multiply - You do it and train someone else.

3. When leaders know how to relate they will discover that there is no one way to lead people. You will have to adopt a style to a group or individual depending on their maturity level, gender and communication style. Our styles should encourage involvement, empowerment and enhance self-worth in others.

4. The Bible mandates that spiritual leaders display a loving, caring and burden-bearing attitude towards others (Galatians 5:22 & Phil. 2:1-4).

5. When we relate we show support and loyalty to team members. Contributions are respected. People are affirmed and given credit for work well done. Ideas of members receive consideration. Members are kept informed on key issues. We give time to listen. We do not push through our own agendas. There is accountability if something goes wrong. We confront and deal with conflicts in love.

As leaders let us sharpen our relationship skills and endeavour with the help of God's Spirit to make it work in the front line of the battle to win others for Christ.

Reflection

1. How would you want those closest to you to describe how you relate to others as a leader?

2. Which areas of relating to others would you want to improve on to have a dynamic impact on how you lead?

11   Insight on the Art of Influence

On my fiftieth birthday my brother gave me a little book as a birthday gift, entitled, *"The Heart of a Leader"* by the famous author, Ken Blanchard, author of the well known book "The One Minute Manager," On every second page of The Heart of a Leader is a large print quote dealing with the art of influence. I want to take the liberty to give 25 of those quotes to you. These are the ones that have made an impression and have been most helpful in my understanding of leadership. Do yourself a favour and get a copy for your library.

1. Don't wait until people do things exactly right before you praise them. Praise progress.

2. Feedback is the breakfast of champions. It is the most cost-effective strategy for improving performance and instilling satisfaction.

3. None of us is as smart as all of us. This should be a teambuilding principle.

4. What motivates people is what motivates people. What motivates one person may not motivate another.

5. Create raving fans; satisfied customers are not good enough. Are they bragging about you?

6. If you want to know why your people are not performing well, step up to the mirror and take a peek. Help your people succeed in accomplishing their goals.

7. If you want your people to be responsible, be responsive to their needs. They will respond with high quality work.

8. It's more important as a leader to be respected than to be popular. Combine tough with nice.

9. People with humility don't think less of themselves, they just think of themselves less.

10. Sometimes when the numbers look right the decision is still wrong. Find ways to get things into perspective.

11. Take what you do seriously but yourself lightly. Relearn the value of a smile and enjoy your work.

12. Real communication happens when people feel safe. Bring out their magnificence.

13. All good performance starts with clear goals. Help your people know where they are going.

14. People without information cannot act responsibly. People with information are compelled to act responsibly. Trust them with information.

15. Your game is only as good as your practice. People need day-to-day coaching on the field.

16. All empowerment exists in the present moment. Respect the victories of the present.

17. You get from people what you expect. Catch people doing things right.

18. Inquire within. Find time for solitude and introspection. It brings out your creative best.

19. People in organisations need to develop a fascination for what doesn't work. Don't cover up errors and hide mistakes.

20. Choose work you love and you will never have to work a day in your life. Developing a personal mission statement will help you find what it is you enjoy.

21. Never punish a learner. Rather blame yourself and say, "Sorry I didn't make it clear."

22. Consistency isn't behaving the same way all the time but behaving the same way under similar circumstances.

23. The only job security you have today is your commitment to continuous personal improvement.

24. It's surprising how much you can accomplish if you don't care who gets the credit.

25. Servant leadership is more about character than style. Use the best style that will serve the best way.

Reflection

1. Which 5 of the above quotes speak most to you and your life right now? Why?

2. Take a few moments to contemplate how you will implement these in leading others.

Part II

FULFILLING YOUR PERSONAL LEADERSHIP DESTINY

There is no room for cloning when it comes to leadership. God has created us as unique individuals with various abilities, passions, perspectives and skills. This bundle of potential has been providentially packaged for the specific purpose God intends for you as leader. This does not mean we can't look to role models or aspire to be more like leaders we admire. It does prohibit us from becoming a copycat of someone else. This section of reflections takes a look at the various ways in which the act of leadership is played out. Leadership with integrity involves being true to the self that God created. It's a sobering thought to understand that artificially working to be something we are not, or something we need not be, is going against God's will for our leadership. Every spiritual leader has a God-given purpose and all the potential as well as the stuff and style they need to be effective for Him.

12 Will, Purpose, Calling, Gifting, Vision, and Destiny

Being the leader God wants you to be depends on how you understand God's will, purpose, calling, gifting, vision and destiny. Are these terms different words describing the same thing? For many years I agonised over these concepts. Most preachers make God's will, purpose and call sound like the same thing. Often young people ask for help with 'God's will' for their lives. I hear statements like, 'I don't know what God is calling me to do'. I've seen staff confused when they see little fruit for their labours. Focussed reflection on these issues was prompted as my son Brent-David agonised over his study and career options.

Ed Delph has provided some helpful instruction in this regard. I trust that these definitions, will help you as you seek God's best in your ministry and lead others to do the same.

1. **WILL** - The term 'will' is defined as a choice or determination; mandate; intention. God's will then is the total determination, intention and mandate of God for all creation both corporately and individually. Matt. 6:10; Ps. 40:8a; Eph. 1:9a.

2. **PURPOSE** - Purpose is the end or object towards which effort is directed; function or intention. Purpose reflects a reason for being or a reason why effort is being directed. Purpose is more specific than will, but still very broad in its meaning. Purpose implies a reason for being. Myles Munroe says, "Purpose is the original intent in the mind of the creator that motivated him to create a particular item. Purpose is why. Wherever purpose is not known, abuse is inevitable." See Prov. 19:21; 1 John 3:8b

3. **CALLING** - the word 'calling' refers to a vocation, trade or profession. From a biblical point of view the New Testament Dictionary describes call as 'A commission by God'. Calling could be described as who and what you are meant to be. In a corporate sense, calling describes what an organisation should become in order to do what it is supposed to do. The same is true on a personal level. 1 Peter 1:15 reveals that our call comes from God, and that God has a purpose in His calling. Further reference can be made to 1 Peter 2:21, 3:9; Rom. 1:1; 1Cor. 1:2a; Rom. 8:28b.

4. **GIFTS** - God uniquely equips us through gifting. These are from the Holy Spirit and expressed in personality (Rom. 12:3-8), ministry (1 Cor. 12:4-11) or office (Eph. 4:7-16). The gifts of God to us by grace give us the ability as well as the divine right to use them to accomplish our assigned purpose. Simply stated your gifts give you the power to accomplish God's purpose in your life and the life of the church (Rom. 12:6a).

5. **VISION** - Terry Virgo defines vision as 'A compelling picture of a preferable future that motivates one to perform.' Vision is motivational in its essence. Visionaries are people who see a picture of what God wants, and can communicate it in a way that motivates and activates people toward purpose. Vision includes the ability to see the end from the beginning. Vision is the direct result of purpose, providing the impetus to act on the direction set by purpose. Prov. 29:18; Acts 26:19.

6. **DESTINY** - "A pre-determined course of events that has been decreed, assigned and dedicated in advance for a particular purpose or place, so prosperity ultimately occurs," Chuck Pierce. The Apostle Paul uses the term "predestined" in the use of this concept. Destiny is the ultimate place where God wants to get you or your church. It is the 'dream' of God's heart, the ultimate purposes of God. Destiny includes the desired steps that God has for you to get you to His decreed, assigned and dedicated purpose of place - His destination. Rom. 8:30a; Eph. 1:11.

Careful reflection on each of these areas is necessary for the Christian leader that aspires to be the leader God intended. The synergy that comes from a clear understanding of each allows for one to see the bigger picture: the sovereignty of God in your life and preparation for His work.

Reflection

1. Now that you know the definitions, please identify whether you are grappling with God's Will, Purpose, Calling, Gifting, Vision or Destiny in your life.

2. How have you experienced God directing you personally in terms of the above?

13 Discovering yourself

It is critical that leaders are self-aware. I have a file in my cabinet, labelled 'David Kadalie'. I feel like I have done every possible test on myself I could lay my hands on. Truth be told, this discipline has set me free. The more I learn about how God made me the more I discover His purpose for me on this earth. It is now difficult for others to impose their dreams on me or to manipulate me into doing things I know I am not gifted to do.

The leader needs to identify and take into consideration the following personal qualities if they are going to be effective in ministry:

- Talents
- Passion
- Temperament
- Communication style
- Spiritual gifting
- Leadership style
- Personality profile

Discovering ourselves takes education, experimentation, practice and continual evaluation. All of these are crucial for the following leadership tasks:

- Leading a team
- Growing your ministry
- Knowing God's purpose for your life
- Joyful service
- Accountability in ministry.

The following definitions and descriptions will add a bit more insight for the task of increased self-awareness:

Definitions:

- Talents - Natural, special or personal ability. The capacity to do something not many others can do, or do something much better than others can do.

- Passion - Something for which you have a strong liking or enthusiasm. You may have the gift of teaching but your passion could be to specifically teach children.

- Temperament - A person's nature as it affects the way he thinks, feels and behaves. Tim La Haye, in his book, 'The Spirit filled temperament', describes the Sanguine (highly relational, people person, emotional), Choleric (enthusiastic, success driven, energetic), Melancholic (reflective, analytical, introspective) and Phlegmatic temperaments (determined, sober judgement, composed, deliberate).

- Communication style - Duane Elmer gives us the five styles in communication to enable us to communicate with greater sensitivity and accuracy and reduce the potential for miscommunication and alienation. He identifies the action person who communicates the 'what', the process person who communicates the 'how', the people's person who communicates the 'who' and the ideas person who communicates the 'why'. A fifth style namely 'blend' communicates with all and is more versatile.

- Spiritual gift - Spiritual enabling given by the grace of God. In the five lists given in the New Testament there are at least twenty distinct gifts mentioned. (1 Corinthians 12)

- Leadership style - It is the manner of leading. There are many descriptions of leadership styles. One fairly common one identifies the following styles: Laissez-faire, where there is little structure or supervision. Democratic/ participative - where the leader is an advisor and sets structure so that the team may perform and here they are allowed to set their own agenda. Manipulative/inspirational - a hard sell approach where the leader sets the goals with little participation. Benevolent/autocratic - it is structured, with close supervision but the team may contribute. Autocratic/bureaucratic - totally structured, with no participation and autocratic rule.

- Personality profile - There are many different psychological tests available to help you become more aware of aspects of your personality. These can help you measure perceptions of yourself, gaining insights into your strengths, the characteristics of the ideal work environment and your weaknesses and how you need others.

A key concept for these various dimensions is to understand the importance of uniqueness. Leadership growth does not require the possession of particular passions or the development of a particular leadership style or personality. Instead growth involves first being aware of your uniqueness with regards to these dimension. Secondly, understanding the inherent strengths and weaknesses of your characteristics. Finally, maximizing the strengths and minimizing the weaknesses (or excesses) that are a part of your profile.

Reflection

1. What have you done to discover your particular talents, strengths, etc. to equip yourself as a leader?

2. What's your leadership profile? And those in your team?

3. How do you interrelate with the various leadership profiles you encounter?

14 Spiritual Gifts

An important leadership responsibility is to equip followers for the work of the ministry. The work of kingdom service can only be accomplished through the gifts God bestows. Unfortunately, too many serve in ministry without knowing their gifts. I have been blessed by the chance to attend many workshops and seminars on this important topic. I think I have developed a fairly balanced view on the subject. Let me share some of the important lessons I have learned about spiritual gifts.

To ignore spiritual gifts would mean a

- Denial of what Scripture says on the subject
- Denial of God's workings in past revivals
- Denial of the testimony of the Church fathers
- Denial of current church growth reports around the world.

The importance of understanding spiritual gifts

1. They are critical to church growth - Eph. 4:11,12 - the body grows, builds itself up and is held together as each one participates.

2. Understanding the role they play is a pre-requisite to knowing God's will.

- Understanding your gifts leads to logical service according to the gifts you have been given

- Understanding your gifts also leads to freedom in service

    a. Freedom from frustrations

    b. Freedom from false guilt

    c. Freedom from manipulation

    d. Freedom to dream and from useless dreams

3. Knowing your gits can lead to joyful service - especially when you do what you were meant to do.

4. Awareness concerning your gifts makes you accountable to God (1 Pet. 4:7-11) - gifts must be exercised faithfully, with fresh anointing and preparations.

5. Understanding the truth about spiritual gifts brings glory to God

- you never take the credit for yourself because you know it is from God. Talent focuses on yourself but gifts focus on God the Giver.

Key principles regarding the gifts

- The Holy Spirit is the source 1 Cor. 12:11
- The gifts are not natural abilities 1 Cor. 2:1,4
- There is no hierarchy in the gifts 1 Cor. 12:15-27
- The gifts are given for the common good of the body 1 Cor. 12:7
- The gifts are different from the fruit of the Spirit Gal. 5:22,23
- The gifts may come in combinations 2 Tim. 4:1-5
- The gifts are not to be neglected 1 Tim. 4:14, 2 Tim. 1:6
- The gifts must be used generously 1 Cor. 12:4-8

Finding your Spiritual Gift(s)

1. Through education- learn, participate in a gifts workshop, talk to other people, read on the subject

2. Through experimentation - get involved and active with the gifts you are aware of, examine why you are doing what you are doing. 60%-70% of our work should relate to our giftedness.

3. Through evaluation - obtain feedback, check your feelings, especially for irritations. Check the results of your work. See what you like to do. Where you are effective. Do you see fruit and evidence of God's blessings in that area? Get feedback from others. They will confirm the giftedness.

The need for balance regarding gifts 1 Cor. 12

- Some people undervalue themselves and feel they do not belong. This also makes them covet other people's gifts.
- Some again overvalue their gift and make others feel they do not belong. This is a kind of gift projection. When others don't do it, we condemn them.
- Every gift in the Bible should be used in the context of love.

Here is a list of many of the gifts identified in Scripture:

- Apostle
- Prophet
- Evangelist
- Teacher
- Pastor
- Deacon
- Exhortation
- Giving
- Leadership

- Mercy
- Word of wisdom
- Faith
- Word of knowledge
- Healing
- Hospitality
- Miracles
- Discernment
- Tongues

- Interpretation of tongues
- Administration
- Helps
- Celibacy
- Voluntary poverty
- Martyrdom
- Serving
- Speaking
- Intercession

- Craftsmanship
- Singer
- Musician
- Worship
- Leader
- Teacher
- Hospitality
- Exorcism
- Missionary
- Encouragement

Reflection

1. Having gained knowledge on this topic, what are the spiritual gifts you are aware of operating in your life?

2. How will you use your newfound knowledge of spiritual gifts to develop those whom you lead?

15 Ten Leadership Styles

Charles Gordon has written about the importance of identifying and developing your personal style of leadership and knowing how it manifests itself. Understanding your leadership style involves understanding your gift-mix, knowing the strong and weak aspects of your leadership, and how determining your style can complement other team members to create a healthy leadership-mix. When you model yourself on someone else's leadership style you may inhibit your own growth.

Let's have a look at the 10 styles Gordon refers to:

1. **The visionary leader** - they are future orientated and have definite ideas of a preferred destination and a strong desire to communicate that vision. They get people out of a rut and stir them to action.

2. **The directional leader** - they have an uncanny sense of what to do at the crossroads. They are clear thinkers and insightful planners.

3. **The strategic leader** - they know how people think and function. They have an excellent sense of timing, of direction and of planning. They do not cling to the past but plan for the future.

4. **The managerial leader** - they do things right. They chart things in an orderly fashion, set up workable systems, evaluate performance, oversee direction, and make wise use of resources, manpower and finances.

5. **The motivational leader** - they know how to read people and to inspire them and lift morale. They are skillful at discerning people's needs and expectations and encouraging them to bigger challenges.

6. **The shepherding leader** - they capture their followers' hearts by nurturing and loving them. They are pastoral and can develop a loving fellowship and achieve great success.

7. **The team leader** - they know they will need the right people around them to do the right jobs in order to get the right results. They share responsibility and can build high trust, which is a high motivational influence.

8. **The entrepreneurial leader** - they give birth to new ventures and launch new ideas. They are good starters and should eventually give over to those with a managerial or a shepherding style.

9. **The re-engineering leader** - they can take on an organisational mess and orchestrate a turnaround. They help ministries which have lost their way and give them meaningful direction.

10. **The bridge building leader** - they build trust among workers and get them working in 'sync'. They are excellent co-ordinators.

Reflection

1. Which type of Leader do you consider yourself to be?

2. Take some time to ask those closest to you what kind of a Leader they think you are - the results may surprise you.

3. Which of these leadership styles are you surrounded by in your work?

16   The Authentic Leader

There has been some debate in the past on the importance of transparency of the leader in ministry. How open should one be? In the African context this question presents a challenge to the prevailing view that leaders, by virtue of their position, need to remain aloof and distant from their followers. This reflection should help us consider the questions: Is it important that the followers relate to their leader? Do they want the leader to model strengths only or weakness as well as strengths? Should a leader be a voice of authority, or that of a fellow struggler?

My comment in this regard is that too many of us are misrepresenting ourselves in ministry. People may not say it but they want authenticity in leadership. Do we tell people we had a tough week? Do we tell them we had difficulty with a piece of Scripture? Do we share about our struggles at home? Are we willing to take off the leadership masks and share our humanity with our followers? We are not saying that it is required of us to share every defeat, every failing and every struggle without discretion. Nor should we parade our woundedness to all and sundry. But, are we able to say with Paul, "We loved you so much that we were delighted to share with you not only the gospel of God but our lives as well" (1Thess. 2:8).

The following are reasons why we need to be authentic in ministry:

1.   Authenticity is Biblical

The Old and New Testaments reveal a pattern that leaders ought to be open about their weaknesses and struggles. Moses was exhausted before Jethro, David expresses his struggles in the Psalms, Job had doubts and fears, Jeremiah cried. In 1Cor. 2:1-3 Paul admits to the Corinthians that he comes to them in weakness and fear with much trembling. Jesus modelled transparency by crying at Lazarus' funeral and showing His fear before the crucifixion.

2.   Authenticity prevents hypocrisy

People often award us with a high level of spirituality when they have no idea whether we've had a quiet time with God in weeks, have marriage difficulties, struggling to make ends meet, or struggling with addictions. A commitment to authenticity helps us refuse the false image some project onto us and lowers the mask of hypocrisy.

3. Authenticity builds credibility

Many of us were taught to withhold our true selves from those we serve. The idea was that if the realities of our lives became known, we would lose our moral influence and ability to provide spiritual leadership. In reality the opposite is true. You gain credibility when you share where you have struggled.

4. Authenticity fosters openness

When we are honest about our struggles, those to whom we minister grow more comfortable with being honest about their struggles. Ministry begins when leaders create a context in which people can say, "My name is John, and I lost my job". "My name is Sheila and my marriage is falling apart". "My name is Nirina, and my son has been caught for pushing drugs". We take off our masks so others will take off theirs.

Let's not withdraw ourselves from followers so that we give others the impression that we do not need them. Let's strive to be honest about who we are and in so doing give permission to others to do the same.

Reflection

1. What are some of the masks you have to remove in order to be more authentic and honest in your leadership?

2. Name some ways that honest, transparent, authentic leadership will impact the lives of those you lead.

---

17 The Impulsive Leader

The word 'impulsive' is defined as 'a behaviour marked by sudden action that is undertaken without careful thought.' The Bible never hides the weaknesses and limitations of some of the great heroes of our faith. In the Scriptures Peter is depicted as a person who had an impulsive personality. He had a habit of speaking or acting without thinking. If a course of action seemed right, he would pursue it immediately.

In his book, 'Perils of Leadership' Kenneth Prior mentions a few examples of how Peter displayed some of these impulsive traits.

- He was in a boat and went overboard in his eagerness to reach Jesus whom he had just recognised. [Matthew 14:22-23]

- His reaction to the Transfiguration was to say the first thing that came into his head even though he had nothing to say (Mk 9:5,6).

- Peter's impulsive speech made him a tool of the devil as when Jesus had to say to him "Get behind me, Satan! You do not have in mind the things of God, but the things of men". [Matthew 16:23]

There are other incident recorded in scripture about Peter's impulsive behaviour including when he cut off the ear of a soldier and the time he immediately said that he would never allow Jesus to wash his feet. Peter was quick-tempered and at times quite arrogant. If he had strong feelings on a matter then he blurted them out.

Leadership often present the opportunity to act impulsively. Since many leaders are action oriented this danger is real and ever present. Wisdom and experience counsel that we need to temper our impulsive behaviours. This does not take away from the need to be decisive but it does suggest that leaders need to respond rather than react.

The leader should consider the following as a way of managing impulsiveness.

- It is important that quick decisions be as wise as they are speedy.

■ Learn to speak and act after careful thought and sound judgement.

■ Remember impulsive decisions can have far reaching, unintended repercussions can be regretted for a long time.

■ Be careful about additions to programmes, sermons etc on the spur of the moment because of certain feelings. They are not necessarily the promptings of the Holy Spirit.

■ Do not react to those seeking help but rather listen carefully then give due thought to the advice you give.

■ When views are shared which irritate you, do not give way to your feelings but use your mind and respond appropriately.

Reflection

1. How do you distinguish between impulsiveness and quick, wise decision making?

2. If others had to describe how balanced you are in terms of speed in decision making and reduced impulsiveness, what would they say?

---

18   The Impatient Leader

Some of us are too impatient with the people we work with. Personally I have seen traits of impatience with followers show up in my own leadership. I can recall an occasion when some of my staff and I were casually chatting and joking about some of my reactions to the events of the previous week. Their comments regarding my behaviour were not intended to be confrontational, but they were telling. At the end of the day they left and I took stock.

Study of scripture provides an opportunity for honest reflection on this topic. Impatience does not fit the Spirit-filled walk. It should not be part of the life-style of a Christian leader. Patience is a fruit of the Spirit's work within us (Galatians 5:22). To develop the quality of patience in our lives we need to join our lives to Christ (John 15:4, 5).

Impatience is reflected when we:

- Talk louder when things are not done our way.
- Continually look at our watches when someone else is talking.
- When we take on things that others take too long to do.
- When we fail to delegate because 'I can do it faster and better'.

You are not impatient when you confront:

- Laziness
- Bad attitudes
- Idle chatter
- An undisciplined life
- Procrastination patterns
- Childish and irrational behaviours
- Continued lateness

That is part of good leadership.

Illegitimate reasons for being impatient include:

- When we demand from others works that are greater than their abilities

- When we expect others to perform at our level

- When people don't work as fast as we expect them to. "Impatience often develops over the speed at which others do their work". (David. L Hocking in 'Be a leader people follow')

We exercise great patience when we:

- Give people adequate and reasonable time to complete a task.

- Take into consideration people's gifting, abilities and talents before delegating.

- Are committed to do all we can to prevent people from failing.

- Find great pleasure in helping people overcome their weaknesses.

- Are sensitive to cultural differences.

Reflection

1. What would those you lead say regarding how patient you really are as a leader?

2. What can you implement immediately to be more patient in your leadership of others?

19   The 'Busy' Leader

Today many of us who are leaders find ourselves in a 'rat race' and need to pause and reflect on our busyness. The following is a compilation of some wonderful thoughts by Charles Swindoll on the topic of being too busy:

"Don't substitute activity for living, or busyness for meaningful priorities. Busyness ruins relationships. It substitutes shallow frenzy for deep friendships. It promises satisfying dreams but delivers hollow nightmares. Busyness feeds the ego but starves the inner man. It fills a calendar but fractures a family. It cultivates a program but ploughs under priorities.

The One who instructs us to 'be still and know that I am God' must hurt when He witnesses our frantic, compulsive, agitated motions. In place of a quiet, responsive spirit we offer Him an inner washing machine - churning with anxiety, clogged with too much activity, and spilling over with resentment and impatience.

Slow down. First, admit it. You are too busy. Say it to yourself…your family… your friends. Openly and willingly acknowledge that what you are doing is wrong and something must be done - now.

Need to slow down? Here's how: Starting today, refuse every possible activity which isn't absolutely necessary. Sound ruthless? So is the clock. So is your health. Discuss with your family some ways of investing time with them - without the TV…without apologies for playing and laughing and doing nutty, fun things…without gobs of money having to be spent to 'entertain' you. Put first things first. Go back to a friend you've offended by never writing, visiting with, etc. Apologise and let him or her know you're trying to give people more of a priority in life than projects or activities."

We need to look at reasons why we get caught up in this life and cycle of busyness. What factors contribute to becoming too busy. Consider the following:

1. When all our energies are engaged because of a lack of resources, focus and strategy to do the job.

2. When you make all the day-to-day decisions in your operation.

3. When you have become a one-man show in spite of the potential around you.

4. When your time is occupied sorting out problems others have made.

5. When you become a victim of your own success.

6. When you fail to develop an infrastructure that could assimilate and equip people in a growing church or organisation.

7. When you are constantly frustrated with what is happening around you.

8. When you are driven to control, to make decisions and to give orders, holding on to your position at all costs and feeling threatened at the slightest initiative by a subordinate.

9. When you haven't learned a thing about how to grow and develop people around you - instead making everyone dependent on you.

10. When you have a need to please everyone.

11. When power and status is your main motivation

(Ken Blanchard, Bill Hybels and Phil Hodges, 'Leadership by the Book')

At the point where we reach our limit we often find ourselves reflecting on the most fundamental questions of our leadership. What is the purpose of my life? Why do I exist? How do I find meaning? How do I satisfy my need to be significant? Why are my relationships in shambles? How did I get so far in debt? Who am I trying to please, anyway? How did I get caught up in the rat race in the first place? This unhappy state can be avoided by taking action after reflecting on our priorities

Morley also encourages leaders to do the following when they feel too busy:

- Ask the question. "Do you know anyone who has ever won the rat race? ... Upon reflection...we really don't know anyone who has...then why do we compete in an unwinnable race?"

- Get rid of unnecessary baggage. To "throw off everything that hinders and the sin that so easily entangles, and...run with perseverance the race marked out for us" (Hebrews 12:1)

- Start doing 'the new job we were intended to do' and to stop living an impotent life because you are trying to do everything. Start by doing the job you were prompted to do when you first started trusting Christ. "Therefore, if anyone is in Christ, he is a new creation; the old has gone, the new has come" (2 Corinthians 5:17)

Reflection

1. Name some of the recurring complaints from your loved ones regarding your busyness

2. What are you going to do about the things that have been highlighted in No. 1?

3. What will you have to do to cultivate a quiet, responsive spirit?

20   The Optimistic Leader

Some time ago a businessman and proponent of Madagascar's old guard could see or say absolutely nothing positive about the installation of new President. He could only forsee doom. While the country was experiencing the arrival of a new dispensation with new opportunities and challenges, this man was packing up and leaving to invest abroad.

An optimist is a person who is always hopeful and expects the best in all things. Leaders need to have an active optimistic perspective about thee task at hand. After all, leaders are change agents and as such ought to be continually driven by the conviction that things are going to get better. Leaders are people with a healthy and positive attitude.

Many scholars on leadership agree that a positive attitude is critical in determining whether we succeed or fail. If this is true then we need to explore its importance. A good, healthy, positive attitude towards life does not affect society so much as it affects us.

I like John C. Maxwell's description of attitude:

- It is the 'advance man' of our true selves
- Its roots are inward but its fruit is outward
- It is our best friend or our worst enemy
- It is more honest and more consistent than our words
- It is an outward look based on past experience
- It is a thing, which draws people to us or repels them
- It is never content until it is expressed
- It is the librarian of our past
- It is the speaker of our present
- It is the prophet of our future

Leaders are optimists. To effectively communicate your vision you need to be optimistic so that you can inspire others. According to Martin E. Seligman, "Optimists are more realistic than pessimists. Pessimists may be accurate prognosticators simply because they cause their worst scenarios to be fulfilled."

Doug Murren in his book 'Leader Shift' says this about optimistic leaders:

- They have a conviction that the future will have a positive outcome

- They communicate a sense of competency in facing the future

- They view tests and setbacks as problems to be solved and 'courses' in which to learn more in the university of life

If you are fearful of what is to come then it is impossible to come up with workable solutions for the problems you may face in your church or organisation.

The Apostle Paul was an optimistic leader, in spite of setbacks. He states:"But one thing I do: forgetting what lies behind and reaching forward to what lies ahead, I press on toward the goal for the prize of the upward call of God in Christ Jesus" (Philippians 3:14). While imprisoned in Rome he writes,"Rejoice in the Lord always; again I will say rejoice" (Phil 4:4).

When vision and goals are presented positively then new crises become opportunities for greater effectiveness instead of threats.

Denis Waitley states in 'The Winner's Edge',"The real leaders in business, in the professional community, in education, in government, and in the home also seem to draw upon a special cutting edge that separates them from the rest of society. The winner's edge is not in a gifted birth, in a high IQ, or in talent. The winner's edge is in the attitude, not aptitude."

Reflection

1. Are you a pessimist or an optimist? How do you know?

2. How will you cultivate and maintain an attitude of hope for the future, and how will that affect the way in which you are able to lead others?

21 The Charismatic Leader

My wife Denise is one of many who are fans of Tony Blair, the British Prime minister. She finds him articulate, inspirational, poised, authoritative and influential. She may be right. There is a certain aura that accompanies gifted leaders and a magnetic force that either draws or repulses others to their ideas, vision and leadership style. As you go about your daily chores as a leader you are being watched, critiqued and judged.

Charisma is the innate ability to attract others. Some people, like Nelson Mandela, the former president of South Africa, seem to be walking magnets attracting people to them. There is no doubt that Jesus was the greatest charismatic leader that ever lived. Throughout the ages His life and words have transformed millions upon millions. Even to this day men and women everywhere are forced to respond to His claims whether they agree or not.

It is a fact that charismatic leaders influence more people, make more sales, are elected to committees, are promoted and are invited to give speeches. Being charismatic is a part of being an effective leader, especially when the key functions of the particular leadership position are public (e.g. ministry).

Leadership is partly an art and is the result of acquired skills. We can change personal attitudes and behaviours to enhance our charisma, or attractiveness to others. Here are some practical steps to help you.

1. **Look and listen to yourself** - record your public speaking; practice in a mirror, video record yourself and watch yourself speak. This is the best way to deal with some of your public speaking blind spots.

2. **Get out of your comfort zone** - practice being more charismatic with complete strangers - people oblivious of your leadership role or position of authority and wait for their reaction after you have spoken. Let them experience your personality and respond to the signals you send out.

3. **Expand your intellectual horizons and vocabulary** - By having an advanced awareness of your world around you, you become more interesting to people. Keep up with current affairs

so that you can meaningfully contribute to conversations.

4. **Take the time to make others feel important** - Don't over-estimate your own importance. Charismatic leaders make time for others. One of the best ways of developing this is to practice good listening skills. People love to be listened to and love the listener.

5. **Exert your energies towards solutions and positive remarks** - people attracted to negative energy are those who share negative attitudes. Positive energy will only create more positive energy and that is what charisma is all about.

6. **Become a comfortable public speaker** - you will be in a position to influence others, share ideas, entertain, welcome, inform, and inspire others in formal or informal settings.

7. **Raise your personal standard of appearance** - watch your dress codes and personal hygiene factors.

8. **Desire to be the role model others emulate** - people are tired of phonies. A charisma that is coupled with a good character goes a long way.

Remember,

"You can make more friends in two weeks than you can in two years by genuinely getting interested in other people than trying to get other people interested in you" - Dale Carnegie

'Charisma is a silent force that overrides competing influences for attention and makes you appealing to others' - Nancy Hunter Denney

Reflection

1. What are some of the myths about charismatic leadership, and what are the excuses people sometimes use to avoid providing dynamic leadership?

2. Which of the ideas listed above are most difficult for you to implement, and which are easiest? Implement 5 and record the results.

22 The Courageous Leader

The conviction to take correct action in the face of challenge and opposition is what courageous leadership is all about. It has been well said that "Courage is not the absence of fear. Courage is action in the face of fear" (Randy Haverson). Our heroic image of leadership is coloured with the hue of bravely going forward.

The Scriptures are full of courageous leaders like Joshua (be strong and courageous), Daniel, David, Nehemiah, and Paul. Even Jesus can be said to have demonstrated incredible courage. Jesus also taught about courage: Matthew 14:27   the disciples are told to take courage in the midst of fear. John 16:33 the disciples are told to take courage in the midst of tribulation.

"Being courageous does not mean that you act foolishly, but balanced with ethics and reality, it means taking brave decisions" (Kairos)

Below are common characteristics of courageous people:

o   People who are courageous act and take the first step

o   People who are courageous have overcome their fears

o   People who are courageous can shed the old for the new

o   People who are courageous are willing to take risks

o   People who are courageous are true to themselves and not what others want them to be

o   People who are courageous listen to the instincts of their heart

o   People who are courageous believe in their cause

o   People who are courageous have a fearless determination

o   People who are courageous stand firm in spite of opposition

o   People who are courageous declare their convictions

o   People who are courageous speak truth in every situation

o   People who are courageous confront and wrestle with obstacles until they win

o   People who are courageous live out their values

o   People who are courageous make their dreams come alive

o People who are courageous say 'no' when it is easier to say 'yes'.

o People who are courageous tolerate maximum amounts of stress

o People who are courageous take charge of their lives

o People who are courageous have a deep faith in their God

Here is an excerpt from a very helpful article on 'courage'.

"Where you need to go, you have probably never been before and the chances are that not too many people have gone there either. The road is sometimes long, scattered with many challenges and worst of all, it seems incredibly lonely. You will need courage. Many great leaders paid the ultimate price due to the fact that they had the courage to challenge - to be free and the desire to take others with them - Martin Luther King, Gandhi, Jesus Christ, John F. Kennedy, the list is endless. Their courage carried them to their graves. Welcome to the world of leadership." (Kairos International)

Reflection

1. Do you ever feel like giving in or giving up? Do you actually give up, or do you carry on until the matter is settled?

2. Identify some of the situations you are facing which require courage to deal with. What do you do when you feel over-whelmed?

23 The Egotistical Leader

Have you ever heard anyone comment on the fragile nature of one's ego? As a young leader, I remember listening to a talk about the 'fragile male ego', which was especially addressed to pastor's wives. They were given tips on how to handle their husband's egos. While it is helpful to be aware of how we can hurt others feelings lets not feel too sympathetic when it comes to the matter of ego.

It is interesting that something so 'fragile' can become so dominant in the exercise of leadership. Many have suffered under an egocentric (ego-driven) leader. My message on ego would be to encourage leader 'to die to self' because the Scripture says that God opposes the proud and gives grace to the humble". [1 Peter 5:5]

To be a Christian leader you cannot have a big ego. Christian leadership is about humble service. A servant heart cannot co-exist with a big ego. Too many of us in business or in ministry are on ego-trips and need to know the dangers of an ego-filled heart. Our loved ones, staff and teams are suffering today because they cannot keep their egos under control.

At the heart of ego-drive leaders is an overestimation of our significance. As a result we become leaders with a big ego. This monster manifests itself as follows:

o   A big ego is just concerned about self

o   A big ego's goal is earthly success at any cost

o   A big ego will go all-out to preserve its image

o   A big ego forgets that he leads for the benefit of his followers and not vice versa

o   A big ego has a need for applause and credit whenever something has been achieved

o   A big ego's significance is determined by external rewards and not inner peace

o   A big ego is motivated by power and status and will hold on to a leadership position at any cost.

o   A big ego promotes and protects its self-interest as a main focus

o   A big ego always compares and must have more than the next one o   A big ego leads to arrogance and deceit

o   A big ego will refuse to ask for help when in trouble

o   A big ego thinks he or she is spiritually more superior to others.

"Leaders with servant hearts...don't think less of themselves; they just think of themselves less...their primary concern is for spiritual significance rather than earthly success" (Ken Blanchard, Bill Hybels and Phil Hodges says in "Leadership by the Book')

"All pride has competition or comparison at its root". (C.S. Lewis)

Tom Marshall makes this statement in 'Understanding Leadership'. "The evil of pride is that it gives us an exaggerated sense of our own importance or significance compared with other people". He goes on to say that leaders are susceptible to the sin of pride:

1.   Because of the intoxicating effects of wielding power over other people

2.   Because personal vanity feeds on the ability to do or command things that the mass of people cannot do

3.   Because of the deference that is shown to them by other people

4.   Because of the attitude that if I am better, then others are worse. If I am valuable than others have to be worse. If I am superior then others are inferior.

5.   Because of the desire to come out on top and seeing opponents or competitors as 'being beneath me'.

"Everyone who is proud in heart is an abomination to the Lord. Pride goes before destruction and a haughty spirit before a fall" (Proverbs 16:5,18).

"Do not think of yourself more highly than you ought, but rather think of yourself with sober judgement, in accordance with the measure of faith God has given you" (Romans 12:3)

Reflection

1.   How alive and active is your ego, and what are you planning to do to "die to self"?

2.   To what extent would you want to be known as a leader with a servant heart, and what are the necessary changes for that to happen?

Part III

AUTHORITY AND POWER

Perhaps the greatest error a Christian leader can make is the inappropriate use of power or authority. In fact it is on this axis that Jesus distinguishes secular leadership ('the leadership of the Gentiles') and the quality of leadership required for a disciple of Christ Jesus is very direct on this matter:

'You know that the rulers of the Gentiles lord it over them, and their high officials exercise authority over them. **Not so with you**. Instead whoever wants to become great among you must be your servant, and whoever wants to be first must be your slave - just as the Son of Man did not come to be served, but to serve and to give his life as a ransom for many.' Matthew 20:25-28

Influence through service is the path to effective biblical leadership. This is not a weak-spined, wimpy form of leadership subject to the whims and fancies of others. There is a difference between serving people and pleasing people. Serving leadership involves an approach to power and authority that works for the best interest of others while pursing the purposes of God.

24 The Leader's Exercise of Authority

Seeking dominance and status is part of our corrupt nature. All of us need to be aware of this temptation and be kept accountable for our exercise of authority.

In our exercise of authority it is always for the good of others. Biblical authority and servanthood go hand in hand. Jesus, who had the ultimate authority, demonstrated this servanthood attitude to His disciples (John 13:12-17).

Worldly authority has to do with manipulation, belittling, bullying and dictatorship. Geoff Rutter ('Leadership and Management-What the Bible Says') makes this point clear: "The ground is level at the foot of the cross, and the Christian leader's authority does not derive from position, money, information, personal energy or contacts. Nor is Christian leadership a political power game, an opportunity for dominance or carte blanche for exercising control over others."

The effect on followers of abusive authority is damaging. Too many people live with wounded spirits and under constant condemnation, and find it difficult to enter a life of joy and grace because they find themselves enslaved to a system, a leader, or a standard of performance that saps true spiritual life.

Regrettably even Christian leaders, who are to help and equip their followers for work of service, use their spiritual authority to control and dominate others. Often this is an attempt to meet their own needs for importance, power, intimacy or spiritual gratification. The Christian leader should feel comfortable with his or her individuality and have an inner confidence that requires no flattery or constant reassurance about their performance. They do not strive after recognition and resist being placed on a pedestal.

They know they are under authority, and the authority they do have is a delegated authority from the Servant King himself, our Lord and Saviour, Jesus Christ. It is seen in their promotion of others, in their development of successors, in their service to the people, in the way they give credit, in the way they empower their flock and in the way they share responsibility.

According to David Johnson and Jeff VanVonderen in their book "The Subtle Power of Spiritual Abuse", relationships between people in spiritual abusive systems are characterized by the following:

1. Leaders spend a lot of time and energy reminding others of their authority and how everyone else is supposed to submit to it.

2. There is a preoccupation with performance of the members, which forces them to conform instead of being transformed.

3. People's lives are controlled by unspoken rules - like discovering that you can never disagree with your leader or you'll be ignored, questioned or be asked to leave.

4. There is an unbalanced approach to living out the truth of the Christian life by insisting on extremes.

5. The follower finds that it is almost impossible to leave so you can get the help you need.

6. A misplaced sense of loyalty is fostered, demanded and even legislated.

In Geoff Rutter's book [Leadership and Management-What the Bible says], he gives some techniques which a Christian leader can use to dominate instead of lead through service to others:

1. Use your superior knowledge of Scripture to squash the opposition

2. Wrest Scripture out of context to use as a club

3. Threaten to quit if they don't do it your way

4. Seek support for your position by privately lobbying other leaders

5. Be stubborn and hold out for your way until everyone gets tired and gives in

6. Sneak the action through when some of the opposition is out of town

7. Make public announcements of a decision before it's made by the Board; then they will have to do it your way

8. Cut down those who disagree with you in your messages from the pulpit

9. Pull your rank; tell them, "The Lord told me this is the way to do it".

10. Think through all the answers, plan all the programmes, and just tell them what we're going to do. Don't ever open the door for them to think, make suggestions or plan with you.

11. Be the whole show on the platform at every meeting. That way nobody else get a word in. Don't ever ask your people to lead a meeting, pray, read Scripture, teach or anything like that.

God help us to lead the way that disciples of Christ ought to lead.

Reflection

1. In which ways will you have to change your leadership in order to apply godly leadership authority?

2. Which incorrect applications of authority in the organisation you work in will you oppose in order to influence change?

25 Judging Spiritual Leadership

It can be a challenge to discern the spiritual qualities of a potential leader and weigh these against/with the candidates professional qualities (education, experience, etc.). Sometimes the difficulty with mobilising leaders is judging how they are doing spiritually. In our ministry we have sometimes had a tough time finding the calibre of spiritual leadership needed to lead the movement. Sometimes you get a great CV but what is of utmost importance is the quality of a person's walk with God. Professionalism and business acumen is a plus but finding mature spiritual leadership is a must.

How should one judge the spiritual dimension of a leader?

1. Check who gets the glory

Many leaders love placing themselves on a pedestal and find great delight when others shower them with praise. Jesus confronted the religious leaders in Luke 11:43, "Woe to you Pharisees, because you love the most important seats in the synagogues and greeting in the market places". Often our deeds, positions and responsibilities have caused us to be proud, arrogant and puffed up. God gets a 'by the way' acknowledgement for our achievements and success. Following a miraculous healing, Paul and Barnabas quickly dispelled the adulation that was about to be bestowed on them by pointing them to the living God (Acts 14:11-15).

2. Check the source of authority

It is essential that only those who have learnt to place themselves under God's authority and the authority of others be qualified to give leadership with any authority. John Perry in his book 'Christian Leadership', says, "Unless we have first accepted the yoke of Christ and learnt to be led, we can never be fit to lead others". Jesus demonstrated this and was himself under authority. This is what he says, "I have come down from heaven not to do my will but to do the will of Him who sent me" (John 6:38)

3. Check the fruit

Leaders need to have good reputations (1 Tim. 3:1-7; Titus 1:5-9) and their lives must show forth the fruit of what they preach. They should be righteous, focused, wise, respectable, unselfish, generous, hospitable, gentle, patient, teachable, not addicted to wine, self-controlled and manage their households. The Apostle Peter says that even the non-believers must be convinced by your life. "And keep a good conscience so that in the thing in which you are slandered, those who revile your good behaviour in Christ may be put to shame" (1 Peter 3:16).

4. Check the outcomes in the followers

Are the followers inspired and motivated? Do they feel cared for? Do they feel included in the team? Do they feel they have authority to make decisions? Do they feel developed? Do they feel supervised and coached? Do they feel conflicts get resolved quickly? Do they feel part of the strategic thinking? Do they feel they are held accountable? Do they feel they are encouraged to manage other leaders? Do they feel that they can initiate action? Do they feel they are maturing and growing spiritually? The list goes on and on.

5. Check the motivation for service

Some of the greatest examples of leadership are seen in acts of humility and selfless loving care. During the last supper Jesus demonstrated this servant leadership by washing the feet of His disciples and He wants us to follow His example (John 13:4-8). A leader will go the extra mile and exemplify Phil.2: 3-7.

6. Check the manner of operation

The Bible demands orderliness and efficiency in leaders. Administration is part of what God has designed for His body (1 Cor. 12:27-28). This must be seen in any given team if we are going to utilise effectively all the resources entrusted to us. This honours the Lord and is part of Christian stewardship and spiritual leadership. Kenneth O. Gangel writes a chapter 'What Leaders Do' in the book 'Leaders on Leadership' and says, "May He also deliver us from thinking that Bible knowledge and spiritual lifestyle somehow substitute for competence in leading a Christian organisation".

Reflection

1. Honestly assess the maturity level of your own spiritual leadership, and those around you.

2. What are the areas you need to grow in so that your spiritual leadership measures up to a godly standard?

26 Conducting a Spiritual Audit

Regular audits of an organization's financial statement are essential to ensure good management of resources and accountability. There is a similar value to periodically conducting a spiritual audit, particularly for those in leadership positions. Fred Smith, a business executive in Dallas, Texas, has come up with twelve questions to help us assess our spiritual condition.

1. **Am I content with whom I am becoming?** It's important that we be more than we do or have. We must be sure our profession does not consume our person. Are we holding on or moving on? When you leave your title and power, what is left to fill the vacuum?

2. **Am I becoming less religious and more spiritual?** The Pharisees were religious. Christ is spiritual. Much tradition is religious, while relation in Christ is spiritual. Religion is an experience I can control while spirituality is an experience that controls me. Are you experiencing the love of God in a warm and personal way or do you always feel responsible to impress God?

3. **Does my family recognise the authenticity of my spirituality?** If you are growing spiritually, your family will recognise it. The late Bible expositor Stephen Olford told a group of ministers, "My brothers, I am weary of celebrity religion. I have had my share of honours, but when I die, unless my family can say, 'there is something of God in that man', then I will have failed."

4. **Do I have a flow-through philosophy?** Jesus said, "Whoever believes in me, streams of living water will flow from within him" (John 7:38). Am I allowing the blessings I receive to flow through me? If you are blessed with leadership, then that blessing should flow out. List what you are blessed with. Oswald Chambers says, "When we dam the blessings in our life, we become stagnant, cynical and mean-spirited...the freshness is in the flow".

5. **Do I have a quiet center to my life?** Francois Fenelon said, "Peace is what God wants for you no matter what is happening". Are you running on empty or do you have the time to hear the command, "Be still, and know that I am God".

6. **Have I defined my unique ministry?** Do I know what I can

do effectively? Unless you know the things you can do uniquely well, you end up doing many mediocre things just to please others.

7. **Is my prayer life improving?** Are we finding the mind of Christ? Do my decisions have prayer as an integral part, or do I make decisions out of my desires and then immerse them in a sanctimonious sauce I call prayer? Are we praying the prayer of reality?

8. **Have I maintained a genuine awe of God?** Are we able to express the awe of the Almighty in nature or when we see it in the salvation work in a changed life? Is the awe of God growing in me? The awe of God inspires, it overwhelms, it intimidates my humanness and it inspires worship.

9. **Is my humility genuine?** Here are two definitions of humility. "Humility is accepting your strength with gratitude" and "Humility is not denying the power that you have but admitting that the power comes through you, not from you". There is another quote from Fenelon, "Accept the compliment from a worthy person as a comfort of God".

10. **Is my "spiritual feeding" the right diet for me?** Do you have a healthy spiritual menu fitted for your needs? We have different personalities and character traits that need developing and therefore we must find the spiritual feeding that is right for us, using the Scriptures, writings of others, sermons, biographies etc.

11. **Is obedience in small matters built into my reflexes?** Obedience largely determines my relationship with Christ. Good intentions count for little. Do I try to bargain with God or rationalise with him? Do I obey God out of fear or love? Also, how do I handle disobedience? Do I give excuses or confessions? Do I foolishly either carry guilt or try to punish myself for what God alone can forgive - and will?

12. **Do I have joy?** Joy is promised to us. Do we have it? If our relationship with Christ is right we will have it. Does my joy extend into my suffering?

Reflection

1. What area(s) do you want to improve on the most?

2. By improving your spiritual condition, in what ways will your leadership be made more effective?

27 Dysfunctional Patterns in Leadership

Without frequent and honest evaluation of one's leadership, it is possible to fall into patterns of leading that end up creating a lot of damage in the life of an organization and its people. Nobody like to look long at areas where we fail to meet the standard expected. However, ignoring the warning signs and deceiving yourself over time will generate dysfunctional leadership patterns.

While discussing the topic of failure in leadership, Manfred Kets De Vries in 'The Leadership Mystique' describes patterns of leading behaviour that signify the need for intervention. If you suspect that any of these traits reflect your style, then seek help.

1. Conflict avoidance

   These are leaders who have a need to be liked. They constantly seek love and approval. Because of this need, they avoid any kind of conflict and even skirt dealing with conflict in their team. They are people-pleasers and hate making unpleasant decisions. Often they look for others to sort out people problems. This creates an unhealthy climate in the work place.

2. The tyrannisation of subordinates

   These are leaders who engage in abusive behaviour. They are ruthless and vicious. It is important for them to get their own way. When this kind of behaviour continues it triggers the same aggressive response from the subordinates (this is a defence mechanism to avoid anxiety). This can lead to a culture of aggression in an organisation.

3. Micromanagement

   This is a picture of a leader who needs to be in control of everything. They are so detail orientated that they can't let go of control. They are control freaks and have a lack of trust in other people's capabilities and never delegate. They ruin the morale of subordinates, which has a stifling effect on the organisation. People around this kind of leader constantly feel demotivated and uninspired.

4. Manic behaviour

These are leaders who work hard but not very smart. They have boundless energy and push themselves and others to the limit. Because of their hyper activity they don't always know what they are doing. They are always involved in firefighting behaviour and often lose sight of their mandate. While everyone around them has major concerns about the organisation they just keep going their merry way. They are too inward looking and do not give much thought to innovative advancements.

5. Inaccessibility

These are leaders who are so full of self-importance that they have no time for others. It never occurs to them to lead by example. They never have time to listen to their people. They are totally unapproachable. They shield themselves behind secretaries and closed-door policies. They are occasionally seen in high places looking for 'important' people to interact with.

6. Game playing

These are leaders who can only think and talk about themselves. When others talk their attention falters unless they are the subjects of discussion. They claim all the credit and refuse to let their subordinates shine. They must be in the limelight at all times. Their personal goals sway the organisation's goals. They use and abuse people instead of growing and developing them. They experience a high turnover of people and instill mistrust and anxiety in the organisation. They envy anyone that's a threat and therefore have no succession plan in place.

Reflection

1. What are some of the dysfunctional patterns you observe in the leaders around you? How have these affected you personally and what are you planning to do about it?

2. What do you need help with in order for your leadership to be transformed?

28 The Abuse of Power

You don't have to move around too much in Africa to come across abuse of power. Actually, this is probably not only a local issue but a global one as well. I was an observer at a consortium that was determined to expose the abuse of power and riggings during a recent presidential election in Madagascar to the International Tribunal in Geneva. The same day I visited and prayed with a school principal who had just received his marching orders from the Ministry of Education for allowing his teachers and students time off to participate in the process. I have had to give counsel to students who felt totally abused by their rector. We watch and learn from international news networks of the oppression of the marginalized and human rights abuses in other parts of the world.

Africa has a reputation for dictatorial leadership. Many African states have tyrannical regimes. Oppression is the order of the day. News about this continent has always been tainted with coups d'etat and military dictatorship. Opponents are locked up and prominent politicians brutally murdered. Laws are pushed through parliament to secure election victories. A Kenyan Bishop, Henry Okullu on the subject of political power remarked, "Leadership is personalised and this personalisation leads to idolisation of the leader to such an extent that people are made to believe that their rights come from the generosity of their leader. In Africa every ruler becomes an ungazetted king, sitting in an unimpeachable position, ruling supreme and for life."

Sad to say too many Christian ministries in Africa are built on the same instinct to control. One of my staff members remarked that he personally felt that the abuse of power was more acute in churches than in the political arena. Christian workers have observed this in the manipulation and extraction of money from the flock. The imposing of doctrinal views; the excommunication of those who disagree; the immediate transfers of younger pastors to the bush for querying decisions; the wrong notion of those who think that if you are ordained you are 'untouchable'.

There is definitely a misunderstanding of power in many Christian circles. Power has been given by God for the service of mankind. Dietrich Bonhoeffer in 'Disillusioned with your Church.' critically writes, "The man who fashions a visionary ideal of community demands that it be realised by God, by others, and by himself. He enters the community of Christians with demands, sets up his own law, and judges the brethren and God Himself accordingly. He stands adamant, a living reproach to all others in the circle of the brethren. He acts as if he is the creator of the Christian community, as if his dream binds men together."

How do we avoid this trap?

1. **Encourage followers to be hearers and doers of the Word**
   "In a spiritually abusive system, the mindset of the people is that they have little or no capacity to discern God's word themselves…to cause religious performance on the part of the people in order to meet the needs of the leaders, to 'prove' that they and their theology are right…Scripture is employed to bolster the agenda of the person using it". (David Johnson and Jeff Van Vonderen in 'The Subtle Power of Spiritual Abuse')

2. **Appreciate that God has given power for service and not control.** Jesus said, "Whoever wants to become great among you must be your servant" (Matthew 20:26). If you study the gospels then you see that Jesus makes it clear that Christian leadership is grounded in love and that the basis for this is servanthood, which ultimately leads to freedom for all. In Luke 9:54 Jesus says those who are regarded as rulers of the Gentiles "lord it over them, and their high officials exercise authority over them. But you - not so. Instead, whoever wants to be great among you must be your servants, and whoever wants to be the first must be slave of all."

3. **Understand who is in control.** In Geoff Rutter's book 'Leadership and Management' he makes a statement, "True NT leaders cannot pull rank because they do not have any." He also quotes Dr. Louw Alberts: "There are no big shots in the Kingdom of God." Geoff goes on to say: "The ground is level at the foot of the Cross, and the Christian leader's authority does not derive from position, money, information, personal energy or contacts. Nor is Christian leadership a political power game, an opportunity for dominance or carte blanche for exercising control over others".

4. **Assess your motives.** Why are you leading? Is it for the benefit of accomplishing God's purposes on earth through service to
others? Jesus makes it clear that those who seek leadership
must examine their motives (Mark 10:43&44, Luke 22:26).

5. **Rein in your authority.** Remember that this need to rule,
which is inherent in leaders, if it is not under the control of the
Holy Spirit, will lead to dominance, control, abuse, oppression
and tyranny. When it is under the direction of the Spirit of God
it will lead to leadership, servanthood, freedom, development
and empowerment, humility and a people-centred focus.

Reflection

1. To whom are you accountable in your leadership responsibilities?
   Ask those whom you lead to give you feedback on this.

2. How are you going to ensure that your leadership is under the control of the Holy Spirit?

29 Manipulation

I remember a time when I had to deal with a very serious situation of manipulation. I became very alarmed and concerned because one person was in fact keeping a whole institute hostage through their controlling behaviour. It was so blatant and soul destroying that I took the time to do a study on manipulation because many of us in leadership have a tendency to use people for our benefit. Some of us even use prayer, prophecy and the Word of God to manipulate our people into doing things our way instead of allowing them to follow God's directives.

In Genesis 27:43-31:55 we read an account of Laban, a master manipulator. His chief goal in life was to look out for himself and he was willing to use anyone, even his own daughters, to achieve his objectives. According to the commentary in the Life Application Bible, Laban was so shrewd that he "controlled two generations of marriages in the Abrahamic family."

I found two definitions of manipulation, which come from some old YFC training notes.

- "Apply force to situations or to people to engineer circumstances or to influence people in such a way as to achieve one's own anticipated objectives"

- "To gain agreement for one set of purposes that in so doing one achieves a second more important but less visible (hidden) set of objectives or personal agendas"

The dictionary defines manipulation as "Controlling or playing on by artful or unfair means to one's own advantage"

We need to understand how leaders manipulate:

1. The free will of their people is often taken away or diminished. In fact a legalistic spirit prevails. People are not free to explore and to express an opinion or themselves creatively.

2. Their people feel paralyzed and persecuted and live under constant threat, which leads to fear and mistrust. The leader displays an attitude of superiority over their subordinates, preys on their weaknesses and instills an inferiority complex in them.

3. There is almost always anger involved in the manipulation.

4. The leader seems never willing to admit they are wrong but always look for someone to blame or play one person up against the other.

5. The leader uses manipulation as a coping mechanism and way of survival.

6. Individuals are labelled as the problem when they notice or confront an issue.

7. Manipulative leaders become generous or offer special help to those among their people who cooperate. In fact, they buy people.

8. Privileges or rewards are withheld or withdrawn if you do not conform.

9. Indirect communication becomes common. Messages are sent through someone else instead of direct confrontation.

10. They surround themselves with a few like-minded individuals. People they've bought and who are utterly dependent on them.

"It seems hard to believe that Christians, who have answered Jesus' invitation to life and freedom, could so quickly return to a treadmill kind of spirituality that produces soul-deadening weariness." (David Johnson and Jeff Van Vonderen) For many this is true because they have found themselves in an abusive system under manipulative leadership.

Reflection

1. Be willing to be vulnerable and get feedback about your leadership from those you can trust to speak the truth (I have just asked my staff to give me feedback, and trust me, they were honest).

2. Do not resist or be arrogant. If you are a manipulator then you need healing and help. God generously gives His grace to those who know they need it. Peter recognises that God loves His shepherds (leaders) and therefore reminds us to "Cast all your cares upon Him because He cares for you" (1 Peter 5:7). Start casting your cares in the right direction. There is a possibility that you are the victim of a previous manipulative situation and that you have become the very thing you hate.

30 How to Deal with Legalistic, Manipulative and Controlling Leaders

It is a tricky thing to know how to deal with legalistic, manipulative and controlling leaders. Because the battleground is on the field of power, any power imbalance can be cause for an unfair fight. Many lambs have been slaughtered by trying to confront a tyrant. It seems there may be two approaches that one could choose depending on the context. The first is confrontational and the second is relational. Discernment is needed in deciding which strategy to employ.

Consider the approach of Jesus and the Apostles. They witnessed firsthand how people suffered under a legalistic and false religious system. How they were pushed to perform and how people became weary and tired under this oppressive authoritarian kind of leadership. From my study and staff training discussions on the subject it again made me realise the seriousness of this problem. Jesus and the apostles must have faced an acute version of this leadership dilemma and therefore dealt severely with it.

1. They exposed these leaders' true character

Jesus called them:

- 'serpents and vipers' because they were treacherous, spiteful enemies of Christ and the gospel and sapped the spiritual energy of the people (Matt. 12:34; 23:33);

- 'false prophets' and 'ravenous wolves' because they appear to be safe and righteous but lead people astray, robbing them for their own ends (Matt. 7:15):

- 'white washed Sepulchers' because they had a fair outward appearance but inside they were corrupt (Matt. 23:27).

The Apostle Paul called them:

- 'savage wolves' because they injure and corrupt the church, not sparing the flock;

- 'Judaizers,' for spreading their legalistic teachings and insisting on religious performance and good outward impressions to gain spiritual acceptance (Galatians);

- 'dogs', for their malicious barking and biting of the flock; and

- 'evil workers', for degrading the truth by working for the gospel under the cloak of evil (Phil. 3: 2).

The book of Galatians clearly exposes what these leaders are up to. They bring people into mental confusion (1:7), bondage (2:4), place a spell on them (3:1), rob them of blessings (4:15) and hinder them from obeying the truth (5:7).

With this kind of leadership you feel constantly exhausted, guilty and belittled, and you must continuously strive to meet their spiritual expectations. This kind of leadership must be exposed for what it is. Your context could demand a different approach but too many Christians are being hindered in their spiritual walk for us to turn a blind eye.

2. They confronted them and their followers head-on

In Matt. 23 we see how Jesus denounces and condemns the Scribes and Pharisees. Nowhere do we see Jesus so severe in his dealings with the religious leaders. He confronts their hypocrisy, for placing heavy burdens on people, for showing off their authority, for their outward show and form of godliness, for their pride and attitude of superiority, for loving titles and honour and for their idolatry.

Paul is angry as he confronts the Galatians. In Gal. 1: 6-8 he says, "I am astonished that you are so quickly deserting the one who called you by the grace of Christ and are turning to another gospel - which is really no gospel at all. Evidently some people are throwing you into confusion and are trying to pervert the gospel of Christ. But even if we or an angel from heaven should preach a gospel other than the one we preached to you let him be eternally condemned"

3. They told them the truth

You are choosing a fight when you confront this kind of leadership. You will be threatened, resisted, blamed, gossiped about, prohibited from leadership - but keep on telling the truth. A good example is Peter and John's experience in Acts 4:19 and Acts 5: 27-29 where they boldly told the religious leaders that nothing could stop them from telling the truth and showing their allegiance to God rather than man.

The alternate approach begins by recognizing some reasons for their style. Many controlling leaders come from similar backgrounds and know no other way of leading their flock. Their authority is the law and does not come from Christ. Some of them have never experienced the life of joy and grace in Christ. Others come out of legalistic homes and communities. Some are under authoritarian church structures where only the pastor has the ability to 'hear from God'. Others have just lost the joy they once had. As such they are more to be pitied than feared. With much prayer, wisdom and perseverance allow God to use you to break this perversion of true Christianity, so that people can be healed, enter into joyful service and have access to God's unmerited favour.

Some non-threatening suggestions to help such leaders

1. Often these leaders are doctrinally unsound. Find creative ways to bring the truth of God's word to them regarding God's grace, freedom and rest, Biblical authority, true spirituality, integrity, joyful service and Christian leadership.

2. Develop a close friendship with them so that you can earn the right to talk about the issues in a non-threatening kind of way, taking into consideration timing and location.

3. Introduce and expose them to pastors or leaders with a more Biblical style of leadership. Deliberately help to foster these relationships.

4. Sponsor and invite them to attend a good leadership course with you.

5. Slowly and wisely introduce them to books and tapes that will get them thinking, especially from authors and speakers they admire.

If you do not have the strength to continue the effort after trying your best, I want to suggest that you leave or you will take on their traits.

Reflection

1. Identify some legalistic, manipulative leaders you have encountered.

2. How can you be sure that your leadership authority source is in Jesus Christ alone?

3. How will you remedy and eliminate manipulative leadership styles in your organisation?

31 The Status Trap

Status defined *'It is about our ranking or position in society in comparison or in relation to others.'*

Daily I see how status goes hand in hand with leadership. In a poor country like Madagascar achieving a higher status looks attractive to up-and-coming young leaders. But this unfettered pursuit of status alone is worldly and has many potential pitfalls. A close look at this topic made me realise how easy it is for all of us to fall into this trap.

Tom Marshall in 'Understanding Leadership' has the following to say about status:

1. People will sacrifice other worthwhile interests and sometimes accept lower financial rewards just to bask in the status that goes with the job

2. Sometimes status is offered as a substitute for monetary reward

3. Sometimes status is protected at all costs to ensure protocol is observed and recognition is given

4. Status is used to create distance between leaders and followers

5. Some times status is forced upon the people they lead, so he alone is responsible for results

An unhealthy pursuit or attention to the issue of one's status is dangerous.

1. It feeds pride, and fosters vanity and conceit

2. It encourages arrogance and induces leaders to think they are socially superior to others

3. It makes you believe you are successful

4. It makes you hold on to your position at any cost or thinking you'll lose

5. It gives you an exaggerated idea of your own importance

6. It makes you believe that you need to be consulted on all matters of importance

7. You become preoccupied with image and your own reputation

The trappings of status include:

- Titles, special forms of address or distinctive clothes
- Special privileges that others in the organisation do not receive
- Higher monetary rewards
- Even if they speak nonsense, what they say is treated with respect
- It singles out the leader for all success as though he were solely responsible for the achievements
- Access to the leader by ordinary people is strictly limited

You are in the status trap when:

o You maintain a certain aloof distance from ordinary people

o You enjoy special privileges or perks that have nothing to do with the effectiveness of your job

o Your special privilege feeds your vanity and causes conceit and lust after power and prestige

The New Testament picture on this issue

o John 13:12-15: To demonstrate the principle of true leadership, Jesus does a low status job - that of a slave

o Matt 23:5-6: Seeking status makes you a false leader

o Mark 10:40: Positions of prominence are Christ's to give

o John 3:30: Be like John the Baptist, desire for Christ 'to be greater'

o Mark 10:43-45: Greatness comes in serving

o Luke 14:8-11: Always seek the lowest place

Reflection

1. Be honest - how much are you caught up in the status trap, and how are you going to get rid of that way of life?

2. What are some of the status traps in your organisation, and what will you have to do to challenge those?

Part IV

DEVELOPING YOUR LEADERSHIP SKILLS

Leadership can be learned. The pre-requisite for this learning however is a commitment on the part of the leader to personal growth and development. Effective leadership starts at this point. The task of leading requires ongoing learning in order to address the current needs and opportunities. Intentional thought and regular time must be given to understanding how to improve your leadership. The benefits are worth the effort. Your organization benefits from a leader with increased capacity for performance. Your team members and followers benefit from a leader who is resourceful and adds value. You, the leader, benefit from the satisfaction of knowing that you are growing, ready and able to meet the exciting opportunities ahead. Leaders grow themselves first before they grow others and their organization.

32   The Leader as a Learner

Leaders who have made significant progress in life have an unstated motto, 'You're never too smart to learn'. Leaders need to have a passion for personal improvement and must become the champions for others to learn. Stephen Covey remarks in his book, 'The seven habits of highly effective people' that "the best leaders I know are taking an aggressive approach towards their own leadership development." As you, the leader learn and grow you develop a strong desire for both your people and organisation to do the same.

Some things to consider when it comes to the topic of personal development for the leaders:

- All learning does not have to be formal or academic
- Determine the highest priorities for training to improve your leadership and pursue these
- Create a fresh training strategy to accomplish your commitment to personal leadership development
- Place a high priority on the latest research and literature - are you up-to-date?
- Take seriously the fact that an organisation will only grow as fast as its leader(s) grow

Here are ten steps for a leader to be an effective learner:

- o   Recognise where you are now and where you want to be
- o   Decide where to begin and make a start. Don't procrastinate in this critical area.
- o   Set measurable goals
- o   Set an example in order to enthuse others
- o   Seek out the best people and practices to help you become a better leader
- o   Take advantage of free ideas and advice
- o   Gain an outside perspective where possible
- o   Create a learning organisation
- o   Use ministry opportunities to propel learning and reinforce it in daily ministry

o   Make yourself accountable to others for your learning.

"The man who graduates today and stops learning tomorrow is uneducated the day after"

- Author unknown

"Learn as if you would live forever; live as if you would die tomorrow"

-Author unknown

Reflection

1. What practical steps will you take to be a more effective learner?

2. Which areas do you need to learn most in?

---

33   Growing as a Leader

I have watched with pride many of our young leaders in Madagascar receive diplomas and certificates for a multitude of disciplines in their leadership development. Simply observing the learning of others is not acceptable for a leader. As leaders we are often good at telling others how to grow and develop themselves...but someone needs to confront us with the same challenge. The reason is clear. Some of us are in a rut, haven't read a book in years, have lost respect for ourselves, cannot manage our lives, are disqualified to lead and often blame the world for our failures.

Allow me to summarise some of the principles on this topic that I have been meditating on and I now pass them on to you.

1. Be in touch with reality

We all have strengths and weaknesses. Determine what you are good at and spend more time developing that part of your life. Too much energy goes into improving what we're not actually good at.

"It takes far more energy to improve from incompetence to mediocrity than to improve from first rate performance to excellence" (Peter Drucker).

2. Welcome feedback

Find peers or mentors who can honestly tell you what you are doing or failing to do. Stephen Covey has a very simple system that has worked for us. Ask them (our peers/mentors) the following three questions.

- o What do I do that you want me to stop doing? (Stop)
- o What am I not doing that you would like me to start doing? (Start)
- o What am I currently doing that you would like me to continue doing? (Continue)

3. Identify your weaknesses

Deal with anything that will stop you from being the leader you were meant to be. Deal with character flaws or potential character flaws. Start being ruthlessly honest with yourself.

4. Decide to change for good

Stop being in denial and stop rationalising or shifting blame. Accept that you have a problem and that change is needed. Prepare and do something to adjust and to accommodate this change. Take action and deal with things that get in the way of improvements and total transformation.

5. Make your ongoing development a priority

Learn new skills, deal with your attitude, engage your mind, work on character flaws and develop your people skills.

6. Stay current and fresh by learning new things.

About life as a whole, about your job, by asking questions and by seeking answers. Do research and by practising what you learn.

7. Take personal ownership and responsibility for the following:

Your decisions, your destiny, your own growth and your mistakes. Teaching others and leaving a legacy.

8. Hold yourself accountable

This has to do with trust, interaction, support, encouragement, positive criticism, counsel, inspiration, rectification, and sometimes discipline, mentorship and counsel.

"To aspire to leadership is an honourable ambition" (1 Tim 3:1 NEB)

Reflection

1. What are some of the things you will do to make sure that you keep developing and growing as a leader?

2. What measurement system will you put in place to keep track of your growth as a leader?

34   Character Development as a Priority

Too often we bypass the fundamental area of personal leadership development, our character. Character has to do with issues around personal integrity, ethics, values, morality, behaviour and credibility.

Just prior to speaking at a YFC camp I read a book by Aubrey Malphurs, 'The Dynamics of Church Leadership' and decided to check what percentage of my talk on leadership dealt with character and what percentage with ministry skill. Needless to say, I made some adjustments.

Barry Gibbons comments,"Write and publish what you want, but the only missions, values, and ethics that count in your company are those that manifest themselves in the behaviour of all the people, all the time".

Over the years I have painfully discovered the deceptiveness of my own heart and how easy it is to substitute activity and busyness for a life of quality and godliness.

Tom Marshall says,"Leaders always have to work at their character because it is exposed to public scrutiny more than others and will be tested more than others".

In his opening statement on the subject of character development Malphurs says "…the development of godly character is the greatest challenge of ministry but the ministry itself is the greatest adversary of godly character".

Character must precede ministry.

- Character development must come before ministry success
- Our walk with Christ must come before our work for Christ
- Time into my development must come before time into the practice of ministry
- What God does in us must come before what God does through us
- To be with Him must come before to do for Him
- Who I am must come before what I do
- My capacity to be must come before my capacity to do

- Being the object of His grace must come before being the vehicle of His grace

There are many reasons for the prioritization of character:

- Our hearts can be deceptive (Jeremiah 17:9; Psalm 139:23, 24)
- We can so easily seek the leadership office for the wrong reasons (Matthew 20:17-28)
- It is the area that will face the greatest attack (Romans 7 & Galatians 5:16-24)
- It is foundational to Christian leadership (I Timothy 3:1-13; Titus 1:6-9)
- Without it we will struggle with the temptations that come with skill, talents and gifting (Romans 12:3-8)
- It is so easy to slip into a life of hypocrisy and forget that we will have to give an account one day. (Hebrews 4:13)
- We naturally neglect this part and focus on other developments (1 Timothy 4:7-8)
- We will soon discover that strength of character is what will count in the face of dark days (2 Corinthians 4:16-17)

Robert A. Cook said "There is no substitute for character. You can buy brains, but you cannot buy character".

Character development involves:

- A transformed heart and a life of integrity
- Authenticity and transparency
- Daily encounters and intimacy with God
- Accountability and a good reputation
- Consecration and ongoing preparation

Jack W. Hayford has this to say: "The character of a true leader requires an answer to a call that sounds from the highest source and shapes him in the deepest, most personal corners of his soul".

Reflection

1. How much emphasis do you place on character development in your leadership, and what do you consider to be the measure of character?

2. What are some of the events and experiences which have shaped your character and have shown you what your true character is like?

35 Developing Your Personal Leadership Skills

"One of the most universal cravings of our time is for compelling and creative leadership"

- James MacGregor Burns

I would suggest that many recent Christian leadership trends have been a recipe for disaster! Organisations and churches have adopted patterns of ministry and structures which discourage the ongoing development of mature believers and quality leaders. There seems to be a disconnect between leadership readiness, following intentional leadership development, and an appointment to lead. Novices with too little experience are being thrown into the deep end. At the same time potential leaders are either being ignored or regarded as a threat. Also a few willing horses are being overburdened with too many tasks without adequate training or supervision.

Understanding leadership is easier than actually leading. Leadership is a function and not a title or position. It is something you do. Leadership skills and attitudes must therefore be learnt, developed and passed on. This takes time.

What is really expected of leaders?

1. They must set direction and paint pictures of what could be. They are far-sighted (Prov. 29:18).

2. They must be change agents who are willing to be flexible and willing to take risks. The principle of 'change' is found all over Scripture.

3. They must be communicators in order to portray the vision clearly and get the support of their followers.

4. They must be decision makers in order to facilitate change needed to achieve the vision.

5. They must align people by creating a coalition of committed folk serving in areas of administration, finances, management, legal, creative, ministry, etc.

6. They must motivate and inspire in order to keep people focused and moving in the right direction.

7. They must be persistent and continually plough ahead regardless of obstacles.

8. They must be mentors committed to building, equipping and empowering teams (Luke 5:1-11, Mark 3:13-19).

9. They must be role models demonstrating godly, servant leadership and living out what they preach (1Tim. 3).

How a leader can develop their leadership skills

1. Develop a Personal Mission Statement that will answer and portray what you want from your life, your values, your talents and gifts and what you desire to have accomplished.

2. Discover through education, experimentation and constant evaluation your purpose, talents, passion, temperament, spiritual gifting, leadership style and personality profile.

3. Sharpen your people skills

4. Subscribe to leadership publications

5. Get self-instructional packages and videos

6. Make studying an essential and life-long goal in your life

7. Study the great leaders in Scripture

8. Understand Biblical styles of leadership

9. Read biographies or autobiographies of great leaders

10. Give talks on leadership and write papers

11. Take advantage of support services that will help with your leadership development

12. Find a mentor to assist you with personal accountability and growth

13. Annually conduct a personal spiritual audit

14. Take up leadership challenges

15. Invest your experiences and knowledge in others

16. Stay current and read leadership books - build your library

17. Attend regular seminars and do refresher courses

18. Talk to leadership resource people

19. Budget for this development

"To aspire to leadership is an honourable ambition"

- 1 Tim. 3:1

Reflection

1. Consider prayerfully what your personal leadership development goals will be over the next 12 months.

2. Who will hold you accountable for implementing these goals?

3. Budget for those goals to be attained.

36 Delegation - The Answer to Raising Leaders

At one of our YFC Staff Training Institutes in Uganda, a leader confessed, like many, *"I find it very difficult to delegate"*. A definition of delegation is, *"To entrust or commit authority to another as an agent or deputy"*. It is more than just assigning a task to someone. It requires capacity building, empowerment, trust and the freedom to make mistakes. I have found great delight in working with my team members, delegating incredible responsibilities, and observing how wonderfully they performed.

Ken Blanchard, Bill Hybels and Phil Hodges in their book, *'Leadership by the Book'*, state *"...Leaders are willing to share power. Their purpose is to equip other people to become freer, more autonomous, more capable - and therefore more effective."* At times, our insecurities and need for personal power cause us to stifle the development of emerging leaders.

Delegation has its roots in Scripture and there are many principles regarding the topic that can help us to raise leaders. If delegation is done in the correct way it will build morale, give others a sense of responsibility and feeling of privilege.

1. In Genesis God delegates authority to Adam and Eve. In chapters 1:28-30; 2:15, 16, 19, and 20 we see how:

   - God creates the environment for them to exercise their abilities

   - God allows them to become partners in His creation

   - God gives them the responsibility to work and take care of the land

   - God gives them authority 'to rule and to subdue'

   - God holds them accountable for their actions

2. In Exodus 18:13-26 and Numbers 11:10-16 we see that Moses experienced serious personal and administration problems because of the large number of Israelites he was leading. In fact he wasted everyone's time because he was the only one authorised to handle problem cases. His father-in-law rebuked him and gave him wise counsel. This resulted in a selection process of suitable men that eased his burdens and those of his people. He did this:

- By creating a structure - he knew beforehand how they would fit into the scheme of things

- By appointing leaders - he carefully selected a coalition of leaders

- By defining jobs - they knew exactly what was required of them

- By defining his own role - he could now focus on 'leading'.

- By delegating - he gave responsibilities with limited authority

3. In Matt 14, Mark 6, Luke 9, and John 6 in the feeding of the five thousand, Jesus demonstrates how to delegate. He got the disciples:

- To become partners with Him in one of the greatest miracles recorded

- To take up the challenge to find food for this vast crowd.

- To organise them into manageable groups

- To feed them until they were satisfied

- To clean up after the event so nothing was wasted

- To count and record the number of people present

4. Resulting directly from the miraculous church growth in Acts 6 was a multiple of church related problems including discrimination and dissatisfaction. After Pentecost the church grew rapidly and interpersonal problems emerged. The Greek-speaking Jews felt that their widows were neglected in the daily distribution of food. In this situation the Apostles demonstrated principles regarding delegation.

- They acted promptly - they did not wish away or spiritualise the problem, or get involved in sectarian politics, but gave leadership.

- They initiated the decision-making process - we are not always called to make the final decisions but must ensure it happens.

- They involved the people in finding a practical solution - they did not impose an 'already made' decision on the people.

- They determined their own priorities and wisely decided to delegate - this freed them to concentrate on the most important tasks of prayer and preaching instead of getting into 'crisis management' mode.

- They carefully selected leaders to handle the task- they had clear criteria for selecting leaders.

- They publicly presented those who had been chosen to be leaders - I'm sure that this instilled commitment and loyalty, and underscored the seriousness of their appointment.

Reflection

1. Do you delegate, and if so, how well do you delegate?

2. What difficulties do you face in delegating effectively, and how do you plan to overcome these?

3. What would your advice be to a new leader regarding delegation as a tool for raising leaders?

37 Developing your Interpersonal Skills

Effective leadership requires well developed interpersonal skills. This is an area I have always had to work hard at. Interpersonal skills level could be defined as: 'The leader's effectiveness and credibility in relating to others and his or her ability to motivate and influence to get a desired outcome'. Those with interpersonal skills: love to talk to people, are understanding and can handle conflict constructively and with sensitivity

Stephen Covey in the 'Seven habits of highly effective people' shares some important interpersonal skills.

- Helping your teams seek mutual benefits from all human interactions
- Instilling a climate of interdependence
- Placing value on high-trust relationships
- Developing supportive systems
- Agreeing and effectively clarifying and managing expectations and accomplishments.

These are some of the specific areas to focus on in order to build competence in this area.

1. **Initiative** - Being proactive in addressing issues
2. **Assertiveness** - Expressing your feelings • sharing openly about your needs, beliefs, values and ideas
3. **Persistence** - Not giving up or running away from problems; not giving in on a matter of principle
4. **Verbal communication** - the art of: Paraphrasing •Rephrasing •Being empathetic •Active listening •Articulating your thoughts
5. **Written communication** - Effective letter writing • Emailing - Memos •Confirmation •Letters •Minute taking
6. **Negotiating skills** - Establishing your bargaining arena • Deciding on conflict strategies • Planning options - •Anticipating how oppositions would react •Handling conflict constructively and sensitively

7. **Oral presentation** - Considering how you would say what you have planned to say, taking into consideration content, sequence, timing and balance

8. **People focus** - Remembering that people come first and that ministry or business is built on the response of people - Showing sensitivity in handling of people ● Treating your team with respect - Attempting to involve, understand, and be supportive of others

"The way you see people is how you treat people. How you treat people is what they become". Goethe

"We have committed the golden rule to memory; let us now commit it to life."

- Edwin Markham

Reflection

1. Name 3 situations in the past week where you could have responded differently to people and situations around you.

2. How effective are you in terms of your interpersonal competencies and which areas would have to improve for there to be a tangible difference in your organisation?

---

38 Developing Social Skills

In addition to interpersonal skill development, leaders need to take time to develop their social skills. The two are quite related with the difference being skilled at interacting with groups of people as opposed to specific individuals. Social skill assist the leader to be effective in group settings, whether formal or informal. Sometime we confuse social skills with friendliness. I have always regarded myself as someone who could befriend others easily. But recently I was reminded that being friendly does not necessarily mean you have social skills.

A study of the gospels portrays Jesus as someone with incredible social skills.

He could relate to a diverse group of people, religious or not and forged deep and meaningful relationships. His understanding of the customs and traditions of the day made His storytelling go straight to the heart of the matter. Crowds flocked to hear and touch Him and He was known as the defender of children, women, the poor and the sick. Both the clergy and the rich sought his counsel. He had time for family and time to hang out with associates. He felt comfortable both at a wedding and funeral and made Himself handy. Those despised by society became His friends and He went out of His way to meet those rejected. He listened, questioned, cried, gave advice and helped many. People had a sense of hope around Him. Yes, His popularity even resulted in His death.

Socially skilled leaders

1. **Easily** relate to groups of people

2. **Skillfully** get groups to merge relationships.

3. **Deliberately** find common ground with a wide circle of people irrespective of race or creed

4. **Purposely** cultivate meaningful relationships in a group setting and develop a network of friends

5. **Intentionally** enhance the quality of their social contacts

6. **Carefully** influence groups without manipulation

7. **Frequently** become aware of and sensitive to their surroundings

8. **Constantly** make an effort to place themselves in other people's shoes

9. **Regularly** make a great effort to help others

10. **Genuinely** are open to learning new things and other people's ideas

11. **Normally** have a rather optimistic and realistic outlook on life

12. **Surprisingly** have an amazing amount of energy

The most successful leaders have sharpened these important social skills. After all, leaders are in the people business. It is not just about vision, strategies, operations, job descriptions, roles, selection and control. We spend most of our time interacting with people therefore we need to enjoy and learn about this aspect of our work.

Reflection

1. Name the leaders you most admire for their abilities that display these 15 traits.

2. Are you merely friendly or do you have well developed social skills that allow you to influence people?

---

39 Networking with Others

Every now and then I play the keyboard at a local restaurant and teach English to the staff. In return I get a free facility for our training centre and on some occasion the use of the restaurant truck to cart our equipment. Over the years I have developed similar relationships with a few businesses and together we see how we can contribute to each other's enterprises.

These mutually beneficial relationships come out of networking. Networking is the seed bed for partnerships. Networking is communicating with others to create quality, mutually beneficial relationships.

In order to network effectively leaders need to pay attention to the following:

1. Leaders must learn to grow the quality of their contacts and relationships

2. Leaders must learn the importance of each initial contact and discern when to invest networking time

3. Leaders must give intentional thought to building the type of network that will serve their organization

4. Leaders must intentionally follow up first time contacts that seem like they might have good potential

5. Leaders need to learn the principles of networking in order to become proficient in this area

In the book, 'Let your Leadership Speak', James Malinchak has an article on 'Masterful Networking'. He stresses the point that networking is intentional by design.

● You go for quality and not quantity of contacts

● You actively identify what doors to open - not just how many doors

● You place yourself in situations that attract others with whom mutually beneficial relationships can be established

● You take advantage of chance encounters and have faith in the long and short term benefits as you foster relationships

- You do your homework when you are aware of the person you will be meeting - learn what you can about the person

- You should try to be polite when introducing yourself and ask the person how they would like to be addressed

- You should make sure that the focus is on the person you are meeting and not why they should be thrilled to meet you

- You should take the initiative to stay in touch with those you network with

- You should find ways to praise, thank or congratulate them for their accomplishments - make them feel good about themselves

I would like to suggest that:

o Networking will connect you to other opportunities

o Networking will help you discover a world of potential opportunities for your organisation

o Networking will assist you to reach your goals

o Networking will expand the quality of your contacts

o Networking will enhance your leadership abilities

Reflection

1. What interesting networking techniques and relationships have you cultivated, and how do those assist you in your effectiveness as a leader?

2. If you are not yet proficient at intentional networking, which of the suggestions listed will you implement and how?

40 Learning to be an Objective Leader

I am constantly amazed at how subjective I can be at times. Recently we had a brainstorming session and some of us just found it so hard to suspend judgement. Leaders are expected to make decisions on numerous issues and one thing we must recognise is the subjective elements in our makeup that influence our choices.

Objectivity is defined as: The process of making judgements independent of previous experience.

This can relate to career paths, people we ask on staff, friendships we choose, churches we attend, people we greet, restaurants we attend, schools we send our kids to and the way we relate to family or neighbours.

I always thought of myself as a fairly unbiased person but I have come face to face with my own arrogance, prejudices and cultural preferences. Moving to Madagascar forced me to see things a bit differently. Many of the things we encountered were completely foreign to our previous way of seeing things.

We all have our preferences, perceptions, prejudices and specific likes and dislikes. We see things through our own frames of reference and value systems. Our past experiences and motives is a factor in the way we relate to others and act. Many people have influenced us and often we see things through their eyes.

Our subjective bias can cause unfair practices, discrimination and favouritism in the work place. Sometimes we have a language, gender, cultural, norms, educational, political, religious, racial, class and even personality bias. For example we take on staff a person based on one outstanding characteristic, or because he or she is a friend of a friend, or because he or she reflects our value system.

When I read the gospels I am amazed at Jesus. He did not have a prejudiced bone in His body. Some of the folk He related to, some today will call the scum of the earth. His disciples, humanly speaking, were a motley bunch of characters. No wonder the religious leaders had so much trouble with Him. It was not just about the 'heresy' He preached but about the company He kept.

Jesus was objective in His dealings with people and despised the subjective, hypocritical prejudices of the clergy.

o He saw the potential in a prostitute who became a vibrant evangelist (John 4)

o He waited on the Father to show Him His team and low and behold He had to find some of them among the despised (John 17:24; Mark 2:14-16)

o Everyone had equal worth in His eyes - children, women and lepers (Matthew 19:13-15; Mark1:40-42; Luke7:39)

o He went out of His way to meet Zacheaus, that low, lying, tax thief who became Mr. Generous (Luke 19:5-8)

o He took personal interest in a violent lunatic possessed by scores of demons (Mark 5)

o He told a rich man in his face what he can do with his money (Mark10: 21)

o He saw right through the disciples' supposed concern for the poor (Mark 14:4-7)

o He forgave His killers because they were ignorant of their deeds (Luke23:34)

o He took Peter right back into the fold after he messed up big time (John 21:15-17)

I really believe that for us to be objective leaders we need to be spiritually and emotionally mature, sensitive, principle-based and ethical in our dealings with others.

Reflection

1. On a scale of 1 to 10, how objective are you in making leadership decisions? What would you like your rating to be?

2. Consider what it takes to be an objective leader, and consider how dynamic your leadership will be when you make those changes to become one.

41 Learning from Your Failures

I am able to relate sensitively to students who failed at school. I was in a similar position. The saying is so true; "*when we put ourselves in the other person's place, we're less likely to want to put him in his place*". My secretary told me once of a person who tried 9 times to pass the last year of high school. My answer to these young people is simple - 'failing does not mean you are a failure'.

Abraham Lincoln's life illustrates so well how a leader had to contend with failure.

> *In 1832 he ran for the legislature and lost. In 1832 he also lost his job, and wanted to go to law school but could not get in. In 1833 he borrowed some money from a friend to begin a business and by the end of the year he was bankrupt. In 1834 he ran for the state legislature and won. In 1838 he tried to become the Speaker of the state legislature and was defeated. In 1840 he attempted to become elector and lost. In 1843 he ran for Congress and lost. In 1846 he ran for Congress again, he won, went to Washington and did a good job. In 1849 he sought the job of land officer in his home state and was rejected. In 1854 he ran for Senate of the United States and lost. In 1856 he sought the Vice-Presidential nomination at his party's national convention and got less than 100 votes. In 1858 he ran for U.S Senate again, and once again he lost. In 1860 he was elected President of the United States.*

The failings of leaders are all over Scripture. Francis Schaeffer says, "*The Bible portrays its characters as honestly as any debunker, modern cynic or absurdist writer ever could*".

Noah once lay drunk and naked in his tent. *Abraham* the great father of the faith lied a number of times. *Jacob* cheated his brother, *Esau*, out of his birthright. *Moses* lost his temper. *Joshua* opened the way for the awful religious compromise that finally destroyed Israel. *David* was a murderer, liar and an adulterer. *Solomon* became caught in idolatry and his many women brought on his demise. *Elijah* became trapped in deep depression. Paul rebuked *Peter* for refusing to eat with Gentile Christians.

Consider the following perspective on the issue of failure:

1. **Failing does not mean the game is up.** It should not stop you from trying again. For many leaders success came after many fail-

ures. You cannot run away or give up when you have failed. Judas could have had a much different ending. You may be disheartened, disappointed or discouraged but it is not the end of the world. Failing is one of the greatest tools of life. It is part of the process by which you develop as a leader. Elbert Hubbard says, "There is no failure except in no longer trying".

2. **Failing does not need to mean misery for others.** Don't allow your response to failure to become a burden on others. Some relationships suffer because we don't know how to handle our failure. Cast it on Christ, His shoulders are big enough. Peter is talking to the leadership when he says, "Casting all your cares upon Him, for He cares for you" (1 Peter 5:7).

3. **Failing does make you more human.** None of the characters in Scripture were superhuman - yet God used them. Facing up to our failings is essential for all of us, if we are to avoid the danger the Apostle Paul warned of, "Lest after preaching to others I myself should be disqualified" (1 Corinthians 9:27).

4. **Failing does mean its time to take stock.** We need to ask what the cause is so we can deal with the things that cause failure. Is it a lack of discipline? Is it inexperience in the field? Is it an ethical or moral issue? Is it immaturity? Is it self-doubt? Is it the tendency to compare with others? Is it a need for training and the sharpening of skills? You are on the right track when you can trace the reason for your failure. Psalm 26: 2 "Examine me, O lord, and prove me; try my reigns and my heart".

5. **Failing can and does bring good.** It develops principles for living. Out of it can come some of the values on which you base your life and work. In 'failing', God wants to teach, build, make, restore and develop. You can discover that there is meaning and great purpose in life. "And we know that all that happens to us is working for our good if we love God and are fitting into his plans" (Romans 8:28).

A healthy perspective on failure is necessary for the growth and development of a leader. Our mistakes can often teach us valuable lessons about how we can improve.

Reflection

1. What are some of the recurring lessons you have encountered in your failures?

2. How has this affected your leadership development?

Part V

DEVELOPING YOUR PEOPLE

It could well be said that the most important function of leadership is the development and growth of people. Leaders don't really lead organization, business, or ministries - they lead people (in organizations, businesses or ministries). As change agents or influencers it is not surprising that a leader must change, and influence for the good, those they have the privilege of leading. People development is a necessary and continuous take. It takes on several different shapes and methodologies. It must be contextual, it must be relevant and it must, in the end, produce results. A strong commitment to development will help prevent the leader from treating the people in their organization as commodities - there to be spent and used up, and traded or discard when no longer valuable. Productivity is increased as capacity in people is grown. Consider that you can become more productive in the business of making benches if you train carpenters than if you find greater efficiency in bench making. Reproduce your leadership in others - it's the best investment you can make as a leader.

42   The Leader as a Developer of People

I regularly travel to different countries assisting in the development of leaders and strategising for the future development of leaders. It is an essential part of my work, which I enjoy thoroughly.

Any leader worth his or her salt will recognise that members of their team make some form of meaningful contribution. Each one has his or her own distinct personality, coming with a whole range of human characteristics, making them unique yet complex in many ways. *They are the most valuable assets we have.*

If we want effective cohesion and growth we need to understand the challenge of being a developer of these individuals. Investments cannot just be made in materials, equipment and facilities. What will sustain any business, church or organisation over the long haul is a wise and deliberate attempt to invest and develop the available human resource.

John Maxwell in his book 'Laws of Leadership' says, *"A leader is a lot like investing successfully in the stock market. If you hope to make a fortune in a day, you're not going to be successful." He continues, "if you continually invest in leadership development, that is, letting your 'assets' compound, the inevitable result is growth over time."*

David L. Bradford and Allen R. Cohen in their book 'Managing for Excellence' contrasts the model of the leader as a 'developer' with the more current 'heroic' model of leadership. This heroic model is clearly seen in 1 Samuel 8:19-20 when the people demanded a king, *"No, but we are determined to have a king over us, so that we also may be like other nations, and that our king may govern us and go before us and fight our battles".* The underlying assumption in the leader as hero is that the leader is the 'Know it all' with the total responsibility for achieving success. They are involved in everything, handing out jobs and in the constant business of fixing things that go wrong.

This approach to leadership is definitely operating in today's world. Many leaders cannot function effectively unless they are the solo leader functioning out of a heroic image of ministry.

In contrast the 'leader as developer' model involves a twofold purpose for every task:

- The accomplishment of the task
- The growth and development of the people working with him

As an expression of their commitment to others leaders who develop others:

- Learn to have impact without exerting total control
- Are helpful without having all the answers
- Get involved without demanding centrality
- Are powerful without needing to dominate
- Act responsibly without squeezing others out.

Well known author Max DePree has identified three developer roles:

- They remove obstacles that keep their followers from doing their jobs
- They abandon themselves to the strength of others by admitting that leaders cannot know or do everything
- They accept responsibility for the identification, development and nurture of future leaders

A critical measurement of leadership success is the quality and quantity of leaders grown. For the leader who develops people the mindset is described as follows: Leaders don't lead followers, they lead other leaders.

Reflection

1. Which of your own leadership assets will you allow to compound, and how will you go about doing that?

2. Who will you hook onto to develop your leadership?

3. What will you have to change within you to become more effective at developing leaders around you?

43 How Jesus made leaders

In George Barna's book, 'Leaders on Leadership', Leighton Ford describes in his chapter, 'Making Leaders Grow', how Jesus made leaders. He says the test of a leader is that he leaves behind others who have the conviction and the will to carry on. What better model to look at than our Lord and Saviour Jesus Christ.

He called them

Leadership development begins with a call. Jesus found His future leaders fishing by a lake and in other everyday activities. He picked them just as they were. When we call someone in Jesus' name, it is a ministry of powerful affirmation.

He named them

Jesus looked at Peter and said, 'You are Simon, you are going to be Peter'. When we develop leaders we need to know their names, we need to know what their names stand for - that is we need to know them well. Understand their strengths and weaknesses and call them by the new vision of what they will become in Christ.

He made them a team

Jesus believed in teams. He sent them out two by two. Teams accompanied Him. Leadership developers need to know the power of teams. It is important to work with individuals but also to bring them into a group, where strengths and weaknesses can be balanced and vision shared.

He trusted them

He told them to follow Him, then taught them by letting them live with Him and watch Him. He sent them out to go and do, entrusting them with a task. Leaders are made not just by telling them what to do, but also by trusting them to do it.

He tested them

When a big storm came upon them on the lake while they were sleeping on the boat, He asked them, 'where is your faith?'. He pushed them beyond their safe depths. Leaders grow when they are in situations beyond their own control and strengths, where they will learn that they will fail unless they trust in God.

He included them

From the crowds He picked seventy, and from the seventy He selected twelve, and out of the twelve, three. He often took Peter, James and John with Him. To make leaders, we have to focus on the few who have potential, as well as some who may not seem to have it. Sometimes these are risks we must take if we want to grow leaders in depth.

He made them His friends

Jesus' leadership programme was not a formal, hierarchical structure, but a community of friends, and the Friend was the center. The night He left them, He said to them, 'I no longer call you servants...I have called you friends'. Leaders-in-the-making need to sense they are persons, not projects - persons who, in the best sense of the word, are friends.

He warned them and restored them

Jesus warned His disciples of dangers ahead. In Peter's case he warned him that he would betray Him and let Him down. Although Peter denied Jesus three times something turned him around. Jesus gave him a chance and an opportunity to reaffirm his love and his commitment to feed Jesus' sheep. In developing leaders we need to know they will fail. When that happens, they need correction, encouragement and a chance to start again.

He made them understand

At the end it all came together. Jesus disciples realised He had chosen them, prayed for them, died for them and now He was trusting them. He had put Himself in them. Now He was sending them to find His sheep and care for His sheep. Jesus helped them become the leaders He called them to be.

Reflection

1. Who are you leaving behind with the conviction and will to carry on after you are gone?

2. What practical measures will you utilise to make sure they are properly equipped to lead others when you are gone?

44 Releasing Leaders for a Changing World

It is so frustrating to work with leaders who refuse to adapt to new realities, unable to make the necessary changes in thinking and perspective to be relevant (i.e. make a paradigm shift) . Leaders who are effective are those who adapt to change. They are described by George Barna in this manner. "They live in denial of the future, wedded to the past and present, longingly remembering the way things used to be". Our rapidly changing world presents a myriad of challenges to leaders in the 21st Century and demands people in leadership who understand current issues. Those who are not just efficient but who effectively grab hold of the opportunities staring them in the face.

In Madagascar, as in many parts of Africa, we experienced the tension between the new and the old guard. While the country was on the brink of a revolution we had a leadership mentality that seemed to operate on a premise that was steeped in the dark ages. We needed a dynamic leadership that could respond to the crisis and pressures facing today's generation.

The scriptures are full of examples of forward thinking leaders. God chose Moses to deal with the Egyptian crisis, Joshua for the demanding journey into the promised land, John the Baptist to prepare the way for our Lord, Peter to help usher in the church in a Jewish environment, and Paul and his team for the Gentile challenge.

Some of us who have been around for a long time may not have the emotional energy and strength left to deal with the current challenges facing Africa. These include the HIV/AIDS pandemic, leadership crises, poverty and unemployment implications, technological invasion, information explosion, value and idea shifts, global village realities, media influence, Islamic advancements, Satanic onslaught, theological and religious trends, and political chaos. We are too locked into the past and the 'good old days'. We need new leaders who are relevant in the prevailing climate. If God has allowed you to have a good innings maybe now is the time to move on and write your book, but first release the new blood for the new day. Whatever your views on the former President Moi of Kenya, I like his statement, "If I must go, then all those belonging to the old guard must leave with me."

Here are a few thoughtful insights into the need for new leaders:

1. Stephen Covey in his book, 'The Seven Habits of Highly Effective People' says,"The leader is the one who climbs the tallest tree, surveys the entire situation, and yells, "Wrong jungle"...we're often so busy cutting through the undergrowth we don't even realise we're in the wrong jungle".

2. In 'The Purpose Driven Church' by Rick Warren, he comments on Acts 13:36: "David's ministry was both relevant and timely. He served God's purpose (which is eternal and unchanging) in his generation (which was current and changing). He served the timeless in a timely way. He was both orthodox and contemporary, Biblical and relevant."

3. The following excerpt is from Leighton Ford's book, 'Helping Leaders Grow.' "God is already raising up young women and men of vision throughout the world. These emerging leaders are eager to follow the call of Christ. The big question is whether those of us who are now in senior leadership positions will have the vision to nurture them. Will we be like Paul who urged young Timothy to "stir up the gift of God" that was in him (2 Tim.1: 6)? Or will we be like the banyan tree, whose extensive and dense branches do not permit enough sunlight through to nurture its seedlings, so conscious of our own positions and power that we will stunt the young seedlings who are poised to grow into branches? Will they be forced to move away from our shadow to pursue God's call to them?"

4. Elijah knew it was time to step down and hand over to Elisha. Wallace Erickson in his article, 'Transition in Leadership' remarked,"One of the best tests of leadership is the willingness to pass the baton to a successor and let him carry it across the finish line."

5. Instead of releasing, many of us end up stifling and blocking younger talent, who have the vitality, maturity and ability to make significant contributions to the work of the Kingdom. Barnabas recognised Paul as the man for the moment and graciously disappeared into the background.

Reflection

1. To what extent is your leadership geared to a changing world? Talk to those you lead - their answers will reveal a lot about you.

2. What hinders you from developing as a leader today?

3. How will you go about releasing leaders for a changing world?

45 Training, Empowering and Developing Leaders

No church or organisation can say they don't need leaders. We all have seen leaders come and go. Some have either fallen away or just do not finish well. Over the years I had to learn pointers on how to train, empower and develop leaders in order to be effective. A different mindset was needed. As leadership responsibilities increased I found that more of my time had to be spent investing in the development of emerging leaders.

Here are some of the ideas I found helpful for this task:

1. There are some preliminary considerations. We must see training, empowering and developing leaders as a priority. We must see the potential in the ones we train, keep in mind the end product and understand the process it will take.

2. There are questions we must ask. How much are we investing in them? Do we really believe in them? How much time should we spend with them? Do we give them permission to do what we do? Let's also learn to feed their dreams and passion.

3. Some things we must do intentionally. Help them find their purpose. Everyone is a "10" somewhere. We must help them discover where they are "10" and give appropriate training.

4. Help them plan for their future. For some this is hard. Setting goals and reaching them can bring great fulfilment to your developing leaders.

5. Give your leaders permission to dream. Let them succeed and fail. We don't have to do everything right every time. And allow them to think different and to be different.

6. Learn to build confidence and trust in them. Build team spirit and foster faith as you empower them for ministry. This can be done by a timely word, a future focus, a meaningful touch and through giving personalised time.

7. Develop people for Christian life by exposing them to Biblical and theological understanding, prayer and intercession, scripture memorisation and meditation, Godly living, faith and obedience and the Spirit-filled life.

8. Develop your leaders for ministry in evangelism, discipleship,

counselling, motivation and encouragement, equipping and teaching, relationships, spiritual warfare and in social action.

9. Help your people to lead and manage by making them understand the need for vision, strategic thinking, handling change, time management, managing work and people, managing conflict, human resource development, team building, action plans and decision making.

10. Develop materials and resources without reinventing the wheel. Make them transferable, appropriate, progressive and make them meet your needs.

INVEST IN A LEADER AND YOU HAVE A LEGACY

Reflection

1. Which leader that you know will you invest in to leave a legacy and why?

2. What will you do to improve your ability to empower and develop the leaders around you?

46 Spotting the Potentials

There are a number of people I can identify who saw potential in me. I remember my dad encouraging me to play the piano and take on many roles as a youngster in church. Our church Director challenged me to be a youth pastor over 14 churches. The Youth for Christ Cape Town Board believing I should become the first Black Centre Director in the city. The YFCI President appointing me to coordinate our first International Young Leaders conference in Brazil. I can fill this page with names of people who believed in me.

In his book, "Christian Leadership," John Perry gives us a good example in Scripture about spotting a potential leader. The following are extracts from his book.

o Jeremiah was called by God to deliver a special message to an unresponsive, apostate nation. He was really called to be a prophet of both woe and hope in the midst of catastrophe. Neither Jeremiah nor his contemporaries recognised his potential for leadership. Jeremiah always tried to keep out of the limelight. There was no earlier indication that he was to be a prophet but God had other plans. Even though Jeremiah protested God had seen what he could become. That is, God saw his potential, which is clearly evident in Jeremiah 1:5: "Before I formed you in the womb I knew you, before you were born I set you apart, I appointed you as a prophet to the nations".

o Jesus was also quick to see the potential in people. He could see that Simon Peter would become the man of rock. Jesus knew that John the "son of thunder" would one day become the apostle of love.

o We owe a great debt to Barnabas for spotting Paul and for giving him a break. Saul who became Paul was the archenemy of the church and Barnabas had to convince the leaders that Paul's conversion was genuine. For a whole year Barnabas and Paul ministered together and this launched the ministry of Paul. So all that we know and appreciate about the Apostle Paul is because of Barnabas. It is not a wonder that Barnabas was called "the son of encouragement".

For a leader to be able to spot and develop others he or she must be:

1. Secure in their own sense of call and leadership.
2. Constantly on the alert for potential leaders and see it as a priority in order that responsibilities are shared and not dominated by any one person.
3. An example in searching out the potential leaders and investing in them.
4. Willing to take risks with others to help them discover their leadership potential.
5. Ready to allow some whose lives are unsatisfied to pursue new horizons for personal growth and service.
6. Willing to invest time to find and develop others for leadership roles.
7. Constantly in prayer to avoid appointing people into leadership positions that are 'power hungry' or have questionable characters.

Qualities to look for in potential leaders include:

1. Commitment - Do they have a history of keeping commitments and of being reliable?
2. Availability - Do they have the time for personal growth and service?
3. Initiative - Do they show initiative without someone holding their hands?
4. Passion - Do they have a hunger after God and to impact others for the Kingdom?
5. Teachable - Do they show a willingness to learn and an openness to change?
6. Giftedness and aptitude - Do they exhibit a gift for ministry or leadership? Are they good thinkers and do they reflect and act strategically when they get involved?
7. Ability to influence - Do they influence their peers or particular groups?

8. Credibility - Do they earn the respect of others and is there a clear anointing on their life?

9. Trustworthiness - Do they show trustworthiness with responsibilities and resources?

10. Servanthood - Do they exhibit this attitude in their relationships or ministry?

Reflection

1. What prevents you from spotting and developing the potential in others?

2. Give examples of when you spotted and developed the potential of those you lead.

47 Demonstrating Commitment to Your Followers

If general observations are accurate, then many of our followers may be insecure in the workplace, disappointed with the way things are going and stressed out about living with perpetual crisis management. Their dreams are fading or shattered and they are on the verge of burn out. Some are aggravated by the lack of creativity, constant monotonous routines and are in fact 'sleepwalking' through their days. The poet Robert Frost once said, "The brain is a wonderful organ; it starts working the moment you get up in the morning and doesn't stop until you get into office". Many of our followers are practically in 'retirement mode' on the job, and often save their energies for 'after work' activities.

The nature of my work often takes me away from my team and it has taught me one thing - the importance of practically showing my commitment to them. I believe in them and I am certain they will manage the affairs of the office while I am away. This confidence is a return on the investment of commitment I have deposited in their lives. Leadership is and will always be about our followers. They should be a high priority and focus. A constant complaint is that members feel used, abused, manipulated, controlled, pressurised and often underdeveloped. That ought not to be said about those we care and serve with.

We show commitment to our followers when we deliberately:

1. Serve them and make time to be with them

2. Show them a life worth duplicating

3. Stop the 'blame' game and lovingly deal with problems and conflicts

4. Allow them to make decisions in order to gain maturity and experience

5. Give consideration to their ideas and avoid pushing through our personal agendas

6. Release them to take up difficult challenges and to discover their potential

7. Share information with them

8. Empower them and allow them to share power

9. Look for ways to involve them and to collaborate with them

10. Bring out the best in them and show appreciation for work well done

11. Earn their respect and treat them with respect

12. Keep the communication channels open

13. Show support and loyalty

Peter Drucker once made the following statement about an organisation. I would like to make the application to the role of a leader. "The purpose of a 'leader' is to make ordinary people achieve extraordinary things, but in reality most 'leaders' allow even extraordinary people to achieve ordinary things".

People must know that they are needed to fulfil the mission and that they are trusted and valued members of the team. Reading through the gospels clearly shows that Jesus demonstrated this principle with His disciples.

1. He invested intimate and quality time with them, praying, developing and socialising with them

2. They travelled with Him and became ministry partners

3. He helped them form godly values by teaching them the principles of the Kingdom

4. He interceded for them

5. They were an integral part of His succession plan

6. He gave them opportunities for growth and prepared them for 'greater' service

7. He demonstrated to them real humility, grace and transparency

Reflection

1. Name some ways in which you demonstrate faith in your people?

2. Is this part of the culture of your organisation? If not, how will you change that?

48   Helping Leaders Become Competent

Most of my current senior leaders are young people who emerged from within the organization. Over the years I have learnt to have a people development plan as a part of an outcome-based ministry. This made it easier to assess performance. To do this we had to help our staff develop and display Christian character and become competent in certain leadership skills. As much as half of my time spent with emerging leaders was spent doing training of some sorts or collaborating with others to give training. Leadership development is time-intensive but ultimately it pays off. A leader must set aside time to invest in the next generation of leaders so they can be competent to lead their peers.

There are many different skills needed to perform particular jobs. Different roles obviously require different skills. Broadly speaking there are practical, technical, managerial, leadership, ministry, administrative, intellectual or interpersonal skills.

Here is a list of what I consider to be essential skills needed in our ministry. Its quite a long list but it does provide a sense of the range of competencies needed:

o   Computer literacy

o   Typing skills

o   Language ability

o   Numerical ability

o   Mechanical ability

o   Maintenance ability

o   Legal knowledge

o   Project management ability

o   Communication skills

o   Client service

o   Leadership skills

o   Interpersonal skills

o   Management skills

o   Strategic thinking

o   Human Resource processes

o   Labour relations issues

o   Financial systems

o   Conflict management

o   Negotiation processes

o   Evangelism

o   Disciple making

o   Mentoring skills

o   Coaching skills

o   Small group dynamics

o   Preaching and teaching skills

o   Counselling skills

o   Bible skills

o   Youth ministry skills

o   Teambuilding skills

o   Fundraising skills

o   Public Relations skills

Knowing the skills needed is one thing, being able to measure the level of each of these is a further challenge. To assess ability or competency in these areas we need to :

1. Define performance standards for each skill needed

2. Define the required level of performance needed

3. Clarify performance expectations

4. Translate competencies into outcomes

Skill building is an important part of help other to grow. It is helpful to have a deliberate strategy for this area that helps with the development of skills in members of your organization. This development can occur through a variety of different methods:

o   Classroom training

o   On the job training

o   Mentoring and coaching processes

o   Partnerships

o   Working with seasoned leaders

o   Regular assessments and evaluations.

Bill Hybels in his book "Courageous Leadership" makes an interesting statement which I agree with totally. "Leaders are at their best when they are creating a leadership culture...we must identify emerging leaders, invest in them, give them Kingdom responsibilities, and coach them into effectiveness. Then we can each experience the thrill of watching them soar".

Reflection

1. Who do you know who has leadership potential, but who is not yet competent as a leader? What will you do to help them become competent?

2. If you could develop leaders to develop other leaders to develop other leaders, how would that impact on your life, ministry, legacy and organisation?

49   The Leader as a Mentor

Mentorship has become a very important leadership topic. It may be the most effective leadership development method. It is the formal establishment of a apprentice like relationship with an individual for the defined purposes of their growth and development. Much of leadership is caught rather than taught. Mentorship provides a means for imparting to others that which you have a measure of skill or expertise in. Mentoring's current popularity is a part of the increased attention to relational issues in leadership and management that stems from needs arising from today's society's extreme individualism and resulting lack of accountability (Paul D. Stanley &J. Robert Clinton in "Connecting").

For Christians mentoring is rooted in Biblical principles of discipleship. These type of learning and training was quite common in New Testament times. In the Rabbinic and Greek tradition of the Hellenistic period, it was typical for a man to choose a "school" and a "Rabbi" to follow. The man would make the Rabbi his mentor and thus he became a mentee. In the other traditions of the world, the mentees simply subscribed to a school of thought or adhered to the teachings of the mentor. The primary reason for most people to follow a Rabbi in the ancient world was to fulfil personal needs and desires. Essentially, mentoring was about personal enrichment in most cases. In the Hellenistic world, the mentee operated with the hope that one day his own ability and authority would surpass that of his mentor. Typically, this authority came from a deep grasp of the teachings. Jesus mentored a variety of people in a variety of ways. You can see this in Matt. 4:25, Mark 10:3, Luke 14:25,26, Matt. 4:18-22, Luke 6:13, Luke 5:1-11, Mark 3:13-19, Mark 1:21-24 and John 13:1-17

The following is an amplified definition of mentoring:

Mentoring is a relational experience in which one person (mentor) empowers another (mentee) by sharing God-given resources. (Leighton Ford)

Mentor - One who knows or has experienced something

Empowers - Strengthens the capacity to grow, develop and/or change

Mentee - One desiring and receiving the resources from a mentor

Sharing - At an appropriate time and in an appropriate manner

God-given resources - Wisdom, information, experiences, confidence, insight, relationship, status, compassion

"The transforming of ordinary people into apprentices and then into partners begins with the crucial choice, 'I want you in this with me, you and I are going to be partners.' It is a crucial choice that does not guarantee results. It is a choice that must be made with hope and faith. It is a choice that must be made by the leader." (Leighton Ford)

> ### Reflection
>
> 1. Who mentors you and whom do you mentor?
>
> 2. What are some of the most enriching experiences and results you have seen in mentoring or being mentored?
>
> 3. How would you go about being more effective in mentoring?

50   Lessons on Baton Passing

David Bidwell, who was at that time the Africa Director of Ministry Resources and Partnerships, shared a timely devotional during one of our YFC Africa Leaders meetings. It was about passing the baton. It was timely because I had just handed over the YFC leadership reigns to a national leader in Madagascar.

Here are some of the key thoughts he shared with us:

An example of baton passing in Scripture:

In 2 Tim. 2:2 Paul uses the word entrust, or trust with the ministry, to describe what we might call passing the baton. Wallace Erikson, discussing transition in leadership has this to say: "We must entrust the organisation to the right kind of people. Those we are developing ought to be better than we are."

A leader who is moving on may find passing the baton or trusting (entrusting) to be difficult because:

1. The new person has control. The exiting leader will have to give up control of something they once had control over and may wonder what will happen to it?

2. The new person's possible weaknesses/failure may reflect on the departing leader...and those failures, or capacity gaps only seem to appear when the former leader has left.

3. The new person may take the ministry in a new direction that seems to imply comparison: "He didn't take it the best direction when he was here." i.e. the new leader is better.

4. The new leader may now have access to some relationships that at one stage were uniquely the Privilege of the former leader...

    o   "I have to share those relationships now"

    o   "What will be said about me when I am not there?"

    o   "I am no longer the hero"

Facts a leader in transition must face about their successor:

    o   They won't be like me

    o   They won't be perfect

    o   They won't do things the same way

    o   Ultimately, they may prove to be better (bigger vision, better skills, etc.) than I am

The issue of meddling

John C. Maxwell in "The 21 Irrefutable Laws of Leadership" says:

"Walk away from the organisation with integrity. When it is time to leave, walk away without meddling."

Meddling:

1. It demeans the new leader and shows lack of trust

2. It undermines the authority of the new leader (diminishes his leadership among new followers) and sometimes damages the reputation of the new leader

3. Creates confusion on who to follow

There is a fine line between meddling and ongoing mentoring and accountability….the issue is 'control'. If we have passed the baton, when we get involved (if there is a legitimate need) we are under the authority of the new leader.

Therefore when we leave a particular role of leadership:

1. First, give it back to the Lord and believe that He is more concerned about the future of the ministry than we are…then

2. We should direct our input and evaluation to and through our replacement (continue to mentor)

3. We should keep a low profile publicly

4. Any actions we take to assist should be filtered and approved through the new leader

5. We should allow the new leader to answer his own questions about the ministry he leads

6. We must fully allow the new leader to make the decisions that affect the ministry

7. When people who are under the new leadership come to me with a complaint…I get involved only after I have gotten all sides of the story (including that of my replacement) and after I am certain that the complaining person has followed Mt. 18 in attempting to resolve the conflict.

"A leader's lasting value is measured by succession". John Maxwell

Reflection

1. Have you had the opportunity to pass on the baton of leadership? How smoothly did you handle the succession?

2. How easy or difficult is it for you to let go of the reigns of leadership?

3. Describe your understanding of the difference between mentoring and meddling. On which side of the line do you stand, and on which side would you like to stand?

51 Creating Smooth Succession

In an increasingly mobile and changing world leadership change seems to be happening at a faster rate than it used to. It is too bad that more thought hasn't been given to the need for effective leadership transition. Unfortunately there are too many stories of poor transition and calamity that happened during a messy leader change. In my 30 years of ministry I have had no clear direction given to me on this important aspect of leadership. If I had the insight I would have invested more in the future of my leaders. Consequently many of us are unwittingly setting up successors to fail. My memories on this issue are long laborious meetings, urgent prayer sessions, inquisitions and uprooting families, to fill an urgent key position of leadership. Sometimes this was done at great cost. We need to make a deliberate shift in our thinking if we are going to give our organisations or churches opportunities for a smooth succession.

Succession is one of the most important responsibilities of effective leadership. It could be that we would have to change policies and traditions to effectively develop and groom successors.

Peter Drucker states: "*The most critical people decision, and the one hardest to undo, is the succession to the top. It is the most difficult because every such decision is a real gamble. Theretofore it deserves thoughtful attention, wisdom and prayer*".

John C. Maxwell, one of today's greatest champions on leadership has a chapter on this succession in his book, He suggests 5 things that are needed to leave a legacy of succession:

- Lead the organisation with a 'long view'. Have tomorrow and today in mind. Look out for the best interests of the future of the organisation.

- Create a leadership culture. Have strong leaders at every level of the organisation. A succession of leaders must come up within the ranks of the organisation.

- Pay the price today to assure success tomorrow. Every organisation is unique and that dictates what the price will be. There is a sacrifice to be made to ensure lasting success.

- Value team leadership above individual leadership. The larger the organisation, the stronger, larger and deeper the team of leaders need to be.

● Walk away from the organisation with integrity. When it is time to leave, walk away without meddling.

Let me also share some important points as sighted by Wallace Erikson regarding transition in leadership:

● In every succession, the organisation's credibility, momentum, vision and values are at risk. A poor transition can drain corporate energy and resources for years to come.

● The incumbent has a major role to play in this process. It starts the day he steps into his position. He knows the strengths and weaknesses of the organisation and the qualities and capabilities of those who work under him.

● The leader must know when to step down and to pass the baton through honest and extensive self-evaluation. This is a combination of knowing God's plan, understanding your gifting against current realistic needs and the level of satisfaction and support you get from those you lead.

● We must entrust the organisation to the right kind of people. Those we are developing have to be better than we are.

● We need to have a well defined plan for a successor taking into consideration our mission and reason for our existence, the challenges we are going to face the next few years, where we want the organisation to go and therefore the kind of leader we would need.

● This should then lead to the formulation of a job description and profile, stressing non-negotiable qualities, ideal qualities and qualities on which you would be willing to compromise in the leader.

I would suggest that the following leadership qualities are of paramount importance in the identification of successor in a ministry context:

1. Christ likeness - Is he following the Father's will, humble, compassionate, a pray-er, mature with a servant attitude?

2. Character - Do you see moral excellence, trustworthiness,

keeping of promises, integrity and good reputation?

3. Competence - Has he the qualifications, skills, education, training, experience, wisdom, business acumen and maturity to handle the top position in the organisation?

4. Charisma - Has he personal magic of leadership to arouse loyalty or enthusiasm and to build and lead an effective and cohesive organisation? Do his actions and life command respect?

5. Communication skills -Does he express ideas effectively in both speaking and writing?

6. Compatibility - Does he fit the position in the unique culture of the organisation and context?

7. Coachable - Has he a desire to grow and learn with a teachable spirit? Is he receptive to criticism?

8. Commitment - Is he loyal to the organisation with a strong passion and calling? Has he willingness to ride stormy weather and does he have the backing of his wife and children?

Reflection

1. What do you find are the most challenging aspects of creating a "long view" and paying the price of assuring success for the future?

2. How has your view of succession planning been challenged, and how will you go about appointing a successor in your organisation?

52 Placing Others at Centre Stage

The older I get the more I understand Jesus' statement to His disciples, "And greater things you will do". My greatest joy in ministry is seeing individuals in my team shine as they take on greater roles that they never imagined possible. I get even greater joy when they attempt things that I thought impossible. What surprises me more is my preference to stay in the background while they are in the limelight.

There is an element of risk in this. I must admit though, there were times when I miscalculated and placed the wrong person at centre stage that created more embarrassment than pleasure. However if we are committed to developing leaders this is a predictable consequence but well worth the risk provided we continue to be supportive.

Leaders ought to get their greatest pleasure from seeing

- o   Others find their strengths
- o   Growth in individuals
- o   Team members bearing fruit
- o   Their leaders making an impact in the community
- o   Individuals soar and become achievers
- o   Their staff fired up to take on challenges
- o   Their followers take the initiative to revitalise others
- o   Others take over their responsibilities and pet tasks

This principle can be clearly seen in the New Testament

- o   "Each of you should look not only to your own interest but also to the interest of others" Phil 2:4
- o   "Nobody should seek his own good, but the good of others" 1Cor. 10:24
- o   "Let us consider how we may spur each other toward love and good deeds" Hebrews 10:24
- o   "And the things which you've received from me, entrust these to faithful men who will be able to teach others also" 2 Timothy 2:2

'There is something that is much scarce, something rarer than ability. It is the ability to recognise ability' - Robert Half

Consider the process Jesus modelled with His disciples:
- o   He prayerfully and carefully selected His team
- o   He had an intense development plan for them
- o   He discipled, mentored and coached them into effectiveness
- o   He prepared them to rely on God by His Spirit
- o   He showed them the big picture
- o   He released and launched them for greater works

These qualities are necessary
- o   To ensure the importance of leaving a legacy
- o   To empower individuals as they take ownership
- o   To assist in the transformation and development of the individual
- o   To produce fulfilled and satisfied team members
- o   To pass the baton from one leader to the next
- o   To ensure the vision outlives you

This can be achieved through
1. A deliberate discipleship process
2. Good supervision
3. A mentoring culture
4. Effective coaching skills
5. A succession plan

Reflection

1. Are you able to name some leaders who have become who they are by "standing on your shoulders" along the way? If not, name some who will be able to do so within the next 3 years.

2. How easily and actively do you pass the credit onto those who follow you, and how will you improve your ability to do that in future?

53   Raising Leaders through the Ranks

There are many ministries with thousands of followers which do not seem able produce successors. Churches with sound teaching programmes, active congregations, state of the art equipment, and magnificent facilities cannot find someone amongst their own to replace a senior position. Candidates are being brought in from the outside. I think the problem is two-fold. They have no clue about the discipleship process and secondly they think a leader's main function is to produce followers. An important function of a leader is to produce other leaders.

Barnabas' greatest contribution to Christendom was to introduce Paul (Acts 9:26-30; 11:19-30).

o   He believed in Paul before anyone else did

o   He endorsed Paul's leadership to other leaders

o   He empowered Paul to reach his potential (Maxwell Leadership Bible)

You need a deliberate discipleship, mentoring and development strategy that will cost you personal commitment and sacrifice. It's imperative for leaders to unleash and nurture the talent and gifting around them and to create opportunities for them to lead which will eventually catapult them into leadership.

Let me suggest that, in ministry, just creating bigger facilities for more followers could be an image thing, a numbers thing, the easiest thing, a selfish thing or a performance thing.

Why leaders should produce leaders

o   It's a legacy thing - you guarantee future success

o   It's a security thing - only secure leaders give power to others

o   It's an unselfish thing - giving others authority

o   It's a wise-stewardship thing - investment in people

o   It's a discipleship and mentoring thing - a costly process to maturity

o   It's an empowering thing - helping others reach their full potential

o   It's a Biblical thing - the best leadership models in Scripture reproduce leaders. In 2Timothy 2:2 - we are instructed to multiply and Ephesians 4:11-13 - instructs us to prepare people for the work of the ministry.

The wisdom of bringing people through the ranks of your own organisation

1. They are familiar with the ethos and culture of the organisation
2. Their sense of call has been proven and confirmed over time
3. They operate out of first hand experience and not just a knowledge of the organisation
4. They have a better appreciation for the history and culture of the organisation
5. They are the embodiment of what the organisation is all about
6. They have a greater sense of ownership
7. It reduces the cost in terms of time and training in orientating the person for the position
8. There is a better understanding of the person's personal and spiritual journey
9. Relationships have already been established over time
10. They have credibility

The best model is the Apostle Paul's development of his young protégé, Timothy who became the Bishop of Ephesus. Talk about coming through the ranks...

"The truth is that the only way to make yourself indispensable is to make yourself dispensable. In other words, if you are able to continually empower others and help them develop so that they can become capable of taking over your job, you will become so valuable to the organisation that you become dispensable" John C. Maxwell (The Maxwell Leadership Bible).

Reflection

1. How dispensable are you? Do you have a deliberate plan to become dispensable, and when?

2. Name a number of leaders you have developed. How would you go about creating a culture of raising leaders through the ranks in your organisation?

54 Nurturing Our Young to Lead

For six and a half years I worked in a culture where 'youth leader-ship' was an oxymoron. If for some reason a young person took the initiative or led in the presence of an elder he or she had to apolo-gize for assuming that role. In the Scriptures leading has never been about age. God often disregarded traditions to fulfil his purposes. Young people were recognised as leaders long before they had position and titles.

o   David, because he had a tender and gentle heart (1 Samuel 13:14)

o   Samuel, because he learned to hear and heed God's voice (1 Sam 3:17-20)

o   Daniel, because he displayed godly qualities (Daniel 1:8-16)

o   Joseph was an arrogant kid but God saw down the road what he would become (Gen. 37:1-50:22)

o   Timothy because of his reputation (Acts 16:1-5; 1Tim. 4:12)

o   Esther, a young captive Jewish orphan was especially chosen to protect the lineage of the coming Messiah (Esther 2:1-17)

There are a number of reasons why we need to identify and invest in young leaders:

o   They are changing the world

o   They are driving the technological industry

o   They are dictating the music trends

o   They are more computer literate

o   They are dominating the new economy

o   They are influencing and overthrowing governments

o   They are determined to get ahead fast

o   They are curious and becoming the authorities

o   They are motivated by challenges

o   They are more adaptable

"Why focus on these late teens and twenty somethings? Because they are the first young people who are both in a position to change the world, and are actually doing so…For the first time in

history, children are more comfortable, knowledgeable, and literate than their parents about an innovation central to society. The internet has triggered the first industrial revolution in history to be led by the young."(Economist)

What will happen if you do not invest in your young leaders?

1. You will have a leadership vacuum

2. You will lose them to other organisations

3. You will always be looking outside for leadership

4. You will have a lost opportunity to invest in the future

5. You will lose energy

6. Your forward thinking will atrophy

7. You will be out of touch with the present generation

8. You may raise a generation without character

9. You could be the cause of them becoming underachievers

Some radical suggestions for nurturing young leaders:

1. Prayerfully identify the young leaders you need to nurture

2. Have a deliberate strategy to invest in their future

3. Ensure they are represented on every Council or Board

4. Let them set the strategic direction for your ministry

5. Coach them as you give them lots of opportunities to lead

6. Schedule time to listen to them

7. Create an environment where they can be innovative and challenge the status quo

8. Allow them to do what you love doing and more

9. Make sure they have mentors

"If you make them lead they will keep you relevant as they are on the cutting edge and very adaptable. Young people have a healthy naivety. They make changes like no one else will make. They are not hamstrung by all the 'whys' and 'wherefores'." David Wraight

Reflection

1. How comfortable are you with the notion of nurturing young people to lead you and your organisation? Why, and what informs that opinion?

2. Can you think of at least 2 young people you will personally nurture into leadership?

3. How will you make sure that your nurturing of young leaders is handled effectively and responsibly within your organisation?

55   The Issue of Fast Tracking

Developing leaders takes time. There are no short-cuts. I believe firmly that most people who are being fast tracked through a training or development program fall horribly short of the qualities needed to lead a ministry or an organisation. Too many of our organisational dilemmas stem from inadequate and weak orientation and development programmes.

We usually fast track people for one or more of the following reasons:

1. We are desperate to fill a position
2. We hear that we are about to lose that member to another organisation
3. We are under pressure from a higher authority to make changes
4. We do not have an adequate development program
5. We do not have a culture of orientation and development
6. We have always settled for mediocrity and training by default
7. We are not prepared for the investment that is needed to develop leaders
8. We have personally been fast tracked and have no other known model
9. We hear a person is a keen student and eager to learn quickly

Fast tracking could be defined as, 'Causing someone to learn as much as possible in the shortest possible time, for a responsibility that is currently well beyond their present capacity'.

Potential problems with fast tracking someone for a leadership position include the following:

1. Developing skills without character
2. Meeting the needs of the immediate and not necessarily for the long term
3. Developing people who will stay dependant on you
4. Having people in a senior position who cannot cope or do not understand the 'new culture'.
5. Short-circuiting people from reaching their full potential

6. Setting up people for failure

7. Ending up with the wrong person and a difficult process 'to get rid of them'.

8. Having someone in leadership who will never see development and training as a priority.

9. Having a person with a false sense of importance and an inflated ego.

There is a saying that I have used for a number of years. *'The less you know, the more you think you know. The more you know, the more you realise that you don't know'*

We need to assess the following in a development program that gives fruitful evidence over the long haul before appointing leaders

1. Established and acceptable behaviour patterns

2. Foundational truths and principles lived in personal and ministry life.

3. Mature handling of problems, challenges, crisis, conflicts and change.

4. Emergence into the culture (commitment to core values)

5. Submission to leadership

6. Integrity in handling resources and people

7. Understanding of people

8. Understanding of one's profile and gifts

9. The ability to work in and build a team

10. Leadership and management know-how and ability

11. Specialized skills needed for the job.

Reflection

1. Name some of the ways your organisation has been affected by fast tracking.

2. What would have to be put in place to avoid having to fast track people?

3. If you find it necessary to fast track somebody, how will you make sure the process is as thorough as possible?

Part VI

STRATEGIC FOCUS

Leadership effectiveness is enhanced by a clear mind set regarding strategic focus. Leaders give direction. However, before they can do this they need to determine which direction is the best way forward. Vision, mission, purpose, goals and objectives all can assist provided they are current, relevant and well thought out. Organizations that are well led are characterized by a tremendous amount of intentional decision making and action. The leader who lacks strategic focus will soon be in charge of an organization that is drifting, subject to the various external forces surrounding it and unable to propel itself towards a God-given destiny. Focus is seen in the dimensions of planning, decision making, urgency and use of time. This section addresses a number of these important issues.

56   The Leader as a Strategic Planner

Developing a game plan for your organization is an important part of leadership. To do this many successful ministries develop a strategic plan. Sometimes it can take months to comprehensively put down on paper what needs to be done to take on greater challenges, be more productive and operate more efficiently in our work.

The work is well worth the effort provided two important outcomes are realized: the plan is implemented (not shelved), and perhaps more importantly, your leaders learn how to think strategically. The dictionary defines strategy as the process of planning or carrying out a plan in a skillful way. It is the organisation's 'game plan'. Strategic planning is therefore deciding on this game plan.

The Bible has many references that encourage sound planning. I like this one: "Any enterprise is built by wise planning, becomes strong through common sense, and profits wonderfully by keeping abreast of the facts" (Proverbs 24:3-4, TLB)

A good strategic plan normally has behind it a strong team that has worked through a process that includes:

- Vision - What we want to be
- Mission - Why we exist
- Core values - What we believe in
- Objectives - What we want to do/measurable results
- Strategies - Our game plan/how to reach objectives
- Issues - What needs to be addressed to achieve the vision, mission etc.
- Initiatives - The actions to be taken to address these issues
- Outcome - Expected results of our efforts
- Evaluations - Review and revise

People need a plan to move from vision to reality. Many have no clue on how to start. Some prefer the hit and run approach and others complain it is a Western concept.

Jesus had a definite strategy for His life. At the age of twelve He already knew that He was in His Father's business. There were thirty years of preparation for three years of ministry. This included an intensive development plan for twelve disciples, a universal evangelism strategy, the impartation and modelling of Kingdom principles and His death for the salvation of mankind, followed by His victorious resurrection. Before His ascension He placed the finishing touches to His succession plan.

The only way to mobilize your work force and have them function fully is to have a strategy tailored to your organisation. Without a strategy you cannot really accomplish your mission.

- It will help your people understand the reasons for doing what they're actually doing
- It will help you build on those things you do well
- It will help you determine those things that need improvement
- It will allow you to take hold of opportunities that may come your way
- It will cause you to anticipate potential pitfalls
- It facilitates increased understanding
- It speeds up the movement of the business
- It optimises the organisation's energy

Starting the Strategic Planning Process

- Birth your plans in fervent prayer. Prov. 16: 1,3,9 ; Psalm 1:6 ; Psalm 20:4
- Seek out a strategist who could take you through the process
- Link and streamline everything you do in the organisation to your strategic plan
- Use it as a permanent guide to the future of the organisation
- Review on a regular basis
- Have regular reports on key accomplishments
- Be prepared to revise your plan

"Meticulous planning will enable everything you do to appear spontaneous"

- Mark Caine

Reflection

1. What's the strategy for your life, and how far are you in implementing it?

2. How will you go about influencing the direction of your organisation, now that you understand the importance of how to tailor a strategy?

57 A Biblical Exploration of Time

A key strategic decision for a leader is to determine to use their time to maximum effect. It may be one of the most important resources the leader is a steward of. According to Scripture it is a wise person who has the ability to manage his or her time - Proverbs 9: 11, 12. Wise people know the value of time. They take full advantage of every moment.

This was clearly displayed in the life of Jesus. He had time for ordinary people, time for children, His family, time to socialise, time for God's house, time to eat, time to pray, time to teach and time for His life's mission, which was to save mankind and to prepare His team for His departure. Someone counted that the Gospels only record 52 days out of the life of Jesus and yet He could say to the Father," I have finished the work you gave me to do" John 17:4.

The Scripture has many principles in regard to time. Here are a few to consider:

1. **Spend time doing productive things that make you happy.** In Genesis 1:3-27 God created the world just as He wanted it and it gave Him pleasure.

2. **Your time for changing may be running out** (Genesis 6:3) During Noah's time God showed great patience, in fact 120 years - you cannot bargain for additional time.

3. **Time heals many wounds** (Genesis 33:4) Esau and Jacob needed time to realise that their relationship was more important than real estate. At one time Esau wanted to kill his brother for deceiving him.

4. **Guard your time with God** (Ex 16:23) The Israelites were not to work on the Sabbath, not even cook food. God knows that the daily routine could distract us from worshipping Him.

5. **Take out time from your work** (Ex 31:12-17) We need Sabbath or we will lose balance. We need rest from the busyness of life or we could even forget why we are working. Some are even too busy to enjoy their labours or their families. Geoff Rutter says when you ask "what is more important, my family or the Lord's work" remember your family is the Lord's work.

6. **Don't give evil time to influence you** (Numbers 28:1-2)
   God's people had to undergo a period of preparation to
   ensure that their hearts were ready to worship God. That's why
   they had regular offerings and rituals under the supervision of
   Priests. They gave idolatry little time to influence them. Nothing
   had to come between them and God.

7. **Spend more time thinking about eternity** (Ps 39:5-6)
   David realises amassing riches and busily accomplishing
   worldly tasks would make no difference in eternity. In Psalms,
   Proverbs and Ecclesiastes we see the brevity of life.

8. **Understand God's perspective of time** (Ps 75:2) We want
   everything now but God's timing could be different and could
   be better for us. Because of our humanness we cannot com-
   prehend God's time. When God is ready He will do what He
   needs to do. God has His own schedule

9. **Guard against mixing right desires with wrong timing** (1
   Chron 17:1) David wanted to please the Lord by building a
   temple for the ark but God told him to wait. He lived in luxury
   while the ark was in a tent and wanted to change that. He had
   a good desire but had to wait for God's timing.

10. **Time is short and must be maximised**. Let's not neglect
    what is important. Let's be fully stretched in what we are gifted
    to do. Watch procrastination patterns in your life Ps 39:4. Start
    thinking long term.

11. **Make full use of your time**. Need sense of urgency in these
    difficult days - keep standards high, act wisely and do good
    whenever we can Eph 5:15/16. Make full use of every opportu-
    nity.

12. **Take time to make a joyful impact.** This takes a Spirit filled
    life - order comes out of the spirit and brings a joy that will
    affect others (Eph 5:15-21).

13. **Watch spending too much time sleeping**. Poverty creeps on
    us because of laziness - too much sleep will rob you (Proverbs
    6:9-11).

14. **Find time to get your potential out** (Eccl 9:10) or you'll go
    to the grave empty.

15. **Remember now is the time to work** (John 9:4).

16. **Recognise God's timing in your life.** There is a proper time for everything in season Ecc 3:1-8, 11a. Timing in life is important. Discover and appreciate God's timing. Mark 1:35-39

Reflection

1. Identify your greatest time wasters.

2. What will have to change to overcome these?

3. Rate how well you are doing in each of the points listed above on a scale of 1 to 10.

---

58 Timing in Decision Making

Leaders often feel that they are at a crossroad. They must make an important decision based on a number of factors, which include an assessment and evaluation of their leadership. To be more effective and true to their call, they need to consider the future yet take care of the present. There is a tension between the present responsibilities and commitments, and future possibilities and dreams. It's all about making the critical decisions at the right time.

A good leader not only makes good decisions but also makes the right decisions at the right time. Deciding when to move or implement decisions is part of any leader's responsibility.

There are many factors that can make decision making a challenge for a leader.

1. Some events and scenarios are just unforeseen and you are forced to make immediate decisions

2. We go through seasons which demand that we make pivotal or critical decisions

3. Some decisions need data collection and this takes time

4. At times we do not have the information but we are faced with external pressures or deadlines to decide

5. Sometimes opportunities present themselves and you feel they cannot be missed and you must grab them with both hands

6. We live in rapidly changing environment and life is becoming more and more complex.

We have all seen leaders who:

1. Are impulsive or reckless in their decision-making

2. Find decision-making stressful and daunting, and therefore they procrastinate or don't have the courage to be decisive

3. Wait too long before making a decision

4. Assume too much when making a decision

5. Are inconsistent when making decisions - sometimes they get it right sometimes they get it wrong.

6. Make decisions without first informing those it affects

Tom Marshall in 'Understanding Leadership' sees it like this:

"The ability to get the time right is one of the marks of the good leader. The way they do it is less clear. Probably it has to do both with the gathering of data, impressions, cues and hints from the wider than usual span of awareness...when dealing with foresight, the intuitive kind of hunch that comes from discernment and the wisdom that comes from experience."

Yes, it is true that we need:

o To have the facts

o To consider probabilities

o To study trends

o To seek expert opinions

o To do research

o To make choices based on goal

But it is also very important that timing in decision-making be based on:

o Learning to seek guidance and confirmation from the Lord

o Learning to listen to your heart

o Learning to discern situations better and better

o Learning to consider factors relating to your values, purpose and mission

o Learning to seek godly wise counsel from those whose opinions you respect

---

Reflection

1. Identify an occasion when your timing was out.

2. What role does timing play in your daily decision making? Who does it affect?

3. What do you understand to be the difference between "time" and "timing"?

59   The Importance of Passion

Passion is a strong feeling, strong liking or enthusiasm. It comes from the Latin word *passio* which actually referes to *suffering*.' (That is why the suffering of Jesus at the crucifixion is called the passion.) Passion actually describes *an emotion deep in your soul*. People are passionate about many things: politics, sports, issues, ideas and even affairs of the heart. These passions propel us into action causing us to do things that we would perhaps not even consider doing except the overwhelming passion we experience.

A leader will serve their organization well if they have a passion for its vision, mission and purposes. This deep commitment propels them into action, inspiring others to align and work together for the vision. Passion is contagious. It is infectious and brings to life abstract visions of a preferred future.

Passion is seen all over the Scriptures

1. Abraham burnt with passion because of a promise

2. For 14 years Joseph's life went down the tubes but his passionate dream never left him

3. In Ruth's passion we see the power of love

4. John the Baptist was a passionate voice crying in the wilderness

5. Jesus had a passion for souls, that's why "He became obedient unto death, even death on the Cross" (Phil 2:8)

Russell Fraser ('Hillsong') has this to say about passion:

How do you know if you have passion?

o   When you feel you really care about something

o   When deep inside, you own something. You don't say 'the' church but 'my' church

o   When you must find a way to succeed and failure is not an option

o   When you are prepared to sacrifice much

o   When you just love doing the work

- o When you are emotionally involved
- o When you feel very good when things go well
- o When you are not happy to admit defeat
- o When you dream up crazy solutions
- o When your eyes get teary when something works
- o When you get things a little bit out of perspective

Discovering your passion

- o Make sure you're doing what you are called to do
- o Donate some thinking time to do what you've been called to do
- o Don't look for what is humanly possible but for something bigger - the impossible
- o Find passionate friends and talk about your passions
- o Decide to be enthusiastic. It's a decision not a personality type
- o Refuse to be negative and don't let negative people into your inner world
- o Use passionate language eg instead of 'like to' use, 'I love to'. Instead of 'maybe', use 'definitely'
- o Be yourself - not even twins are alike
- o Decide to be amazing
- o Ruthlessly cut out things that make you ineffective - make changes
- o Take risks
- o Don't be obsessed with consequences

George Sweeting described the Apostle Paul's passion for the lost and said,"No trip was too far…no expense was too great…no suffering was too intense…no sacrifice was too deep if a soul could be won." Now that is passion.

Stephen Covey in his book 'First Things First' says,"when we talk about 'the passion for vision' we're talking about a deep sustained energy that comes from a comprehensive, principle-based, need-based, endowment-based 'seeing' that goes beyond chronos and even kairos"

Release the passion of God in your life so that your dreams can come true.

Reflection

1. What are you passionate about?

2. What hinders some of your passions from being released, and what must happen for this to change?

60 Focusing on the Important

My wife is fond of the quote, "What's worth doing is worth doing well". But William Oncken Jr. has made a slight alteration to that quote, "Things not worth doing are not worth doing well". He argues that it did not make sense for people to be efficient at doing what they shouldn't be doing in the first place. It is so easy for important things, for example relationships, to suffer because of the urgent things of the moment.

As I was pondering over this quote, some incidences in Scripture came to mind.

- In John 3: 27-30 John had to withstand pressure from his disciples because of their jealousy over Jesus' growing popularity. John had a job to do and that was to point people to Christ. He had a clear-cut role - to make Jesus successful and then to disappear from the scene.

- In John 7: 3-8 Jesus' brothers urged Him to go public with His miracles in order to convince the crowd. Jesus had His own timing for public ministry and withstood pressure from sceptical family members.

- In John 11: 5-7 Jesus did not respond promptly to Mary and Martha's request to come to their brother's sick bed. Instead He came two days later because He had His own timetable and a definite purpose, which was to raise a dead body and not a diseased one.

- Geoff Rutter, in his book, 'Leadership and Management - what the Bible says' notes Jesus' priorities. "He divided His energy among the many and the few, in line with His strategy of saving the sheep (crowds) and building up the under-shepherds (the disciples)".

Often we are too busy with things that:

- o   Seem to be extremely urgent
- o   Are other people's priorities
- o   Others can do better
- o   Are not important at all
- o   Seem to be the popular thing to do

o   We are pressurised into doing

o   Gives us an adrenaline rush

o   Bring recognition and validation

An effective leader must ask, "What are the important things I am expected to do?"

Stephen Covey in his book, 'First Thing First' has a great quote, "Anything less than a conscious commitment to the important is an unconscious commitment to the unimportant." He quotes answers from thousands of people to the question, "What is the one activity that you know if you did superbly well and consistently would have significant positive results in your personal, professional and work life?" A great majority of folk cited seven key activities.

1.   Improving communications with people

2.   Better preparation

3.   Better planning and organising

4.   Taking better care of self

5.   Seizing new opportunities

6.   Personal development

7.   Empowerment

These are some important things that we don't usually do because they are not urgent. But unless we act on these things they will never really happen.

If you want to be reminded about the things you should be doing today then:

● Re-examine your call, purpose and gifting

● Define your important roles in life eg father, wife, leader, etc

● Look at your job description

● Re-examine your personal and work/ministry goals

● Check out your key result areas

If you don't have some of the above, then you have work ahead.

"Be very careful, then, how you live not as unwise but as wise" (Eph.5: 1).

Reflection

1. What usually sidetracks you from important things?

2. What must change for you to focus on important things?

3. What one thing, if you did it consistently and superbly well, would make you a more effective leader?

61 Saying 'NO' to be Focused

From time to time I disappoint people by saying 'No'.

Many of us were led to believe that if someone asks politely for something, then we should not refuse. Sometimes this is because of our cultural tradition, and sometimes it is because we don't feel we have a choice. There are other reasons why leaders are unable to say 'No':

- It makes them feel guilty - they do not want to offend others
- It makes them look uncaring, selfish and lazy- many have a deep desire to be liked
- It makes them feel needed and accepted by others - especially those suffering from a low self-esteem
- It makes them overrate their own sense of importance - it feeds their egos and makes them feel indispensable

There are good reasons for saying 'No'. Many leaders are able to say 'no' for the following reasons:

- They are already passionate and focused about something
- They know their limits and how much they can do effectively
- They know what they want and what is important to them
- They are weighing the cost in time and money
- They are not prepared to live out other people's priorities
- They are not a dumping ground for things others are not prepared to do
- They are realistic and honest
- They are not overly concerned if it causes an offence

'You cannot protect your priorities unless you learn to decline, tactfully but firmly, every request that does not contribute to the achievement of your goals.' Edwin C. Bliss

It is not wrong to say no

- To someone who wants to distract you from your goals or commitments
- To something that you do not feel strongly about

- Because you do not see the need to be involved in everything others are involved with.

- To something you have very little time and energy for

- Because you would rather do something you enjoy doing

'One element of an effective ministry is saying no - realising that God is not holding us responsible for an entire world' Anitra Rasmussen

We cannot do everything. Many have tried and have shortened their lives prematurely. We cannot accept every assignment, social obligation, invitation, urgent request or opportunity. Our work is important but so is the rest of our life. We need time to make informed, rational and enlightened decisions that are right for us and that will take into consideration important things like self, family, friends, health, reflection, planning, studies, our faith, reading, thinking and fun. Saying yes to everything results in being spread too thin and being unable to fulfil your purpose and calling. It also brings unnecessary stress on ourselves and the ones we love.

You cannot always decline a job or request. But if it conflicts with your goals and priorities, suggest alternatives with your boss or supervisor. Saying no is not an excuse for laziness or to get out of a difficult assignment but rather to be more productive with your time and to focus on important matters.

In Col. 4: 5 the Bible admonishes us to "Make the best possible use of your time" and Eph. 5: 15 challenges us to "Look carefully then how you walk, not as unwise men but as wise, making the most of the time, because the days are evil"

Reflection

1. How easy or how difficult is it for you to say "no"? What motivates you to not say "no" when you know you should?

2. Think of times when you should have said "no". How would you approach those instances differently?

62 Following Through on Your Projects or Intentions

Good plans and intentions are just the beginning. Even building the resources base and capacity for action is just the start. Action must persist through to the end for dreams to become reality.

On occasion I have been fortunate to be the recipient of significant equipping resources for use in the field. I recall once commending our Director for International Ministries for all the resources he and his team had so amicably produced for our General Assembly. I remembered how appreciative we were when they were given… but then I began to wonder..

- Will these get down to the people at grassroots?
- Will they make a difference and help with the implementation of our strategic focus?
- Will lives be transformed because of this effort?
- Will they be shared with the relevant team members?
- Will they go into a file or box to be forgotten till the next gathering?
- Will they only be displayed in the leader's library and be an addition to his already wonderful collection of files and books he has collected over the years?

Our leader at the time, President David Wraight, shared these thoughts with me about following through:

> *"In Youth for Christ we sought the Lord for years to provide resources. God has provided and now we have an obligation to follow through. Too often we make promises and never follow through on our commitments. It is dishonest and deceptive to say we are going to do something when we have no plan to follow through. It is a discouragement to those who sacrifice and deliver to help us in our endeavours when they see no fruit down the road. Failing to follow through attacks our self image, because it makes us ineffective."*

Follow through can be described as the ability to carry a project or intention to its full completion; bring to a finish or end; enforce what we say; carry out a plan without deviation; action and operation.

Follow through is a critical skill that is needed for leaders and managers. When you are poor at follow through, you:

- Botch projects
- Break trust
- Waste money
- Waste time
- Impact relationships negatively
- Become a bottle-neck in the organisation

Failure to follow through results from

- Communication breakdown
- Disconnect between the person initiating the project and the one implementing it
- People who are confused about priorities
- People who are asked to do more and more with less and less
- When at the beginning everyone is excited until the next best thing comes along (an attention deficit ministry)

Here are some thoughts on how to be effective in the area of follow through:

- Realise it requires energy and involvement
- It needs a specific personality and skills
- You'll need to get your thoughts and activities well organised
- Keep task lists
- Hold regular meetings
- Learn how to delegate
- Take time out to reflect
- Do not operate in crisis mode
- Know who needs to be in the loop
- Have a fundamental desire to complete things
- Watch the busy syndrome
- Don't commit yourself to things you know you cannot deliver on

- Develop an assessment tool to determine follow through
- Make it an integral part of your culture

Reflection

1. What are some of the negative outcomes you have seen when follow through is absent?

2. Rate your own effectiveness in following through to completion, and state how you will improve in this area.

---

63 Understanding Procrastination

Procrastination simply means putting off things until another time. It is the avoidance of starting a task or not seeing it to its conclusion. Kenneth A. Erickson in his book "Christian Time Management" suggests that the Apostle Paul could have faced this challenge when he wrote in Romans 7:18-19, *"Though the will to do good is there, the deed is not. The good which I want to do, I fail to do"* (NEB).

We procrastinate in many different areas, on projects, studies, family commitments, assignments etc. H.G. Bohn describes this tendency so accurately, "One of these days soon becomes none of these days". With his tongue in his cheek, Edwin C. Bliss says, "If procrastination is your problem, don't put off doing something about it".

Some of us struggle with procrastination

- o Because of our workload and over scheduling
- o Because of parents who did everything for us
- o Because we just can't seem to get things done or to implement tasks
- o Because of ill health and constant fatigue
- o Because of confused priorities
- o Because of over commitments
- o Because some tasks seem too difficult and overpowering
- o Because we wait for flashes of inspiration before taking action
- o Because we avoid unpleasant tasks
- o Because of doing big tasks all at once
- o Because of poor concentration
- o Because of a lack of basic management principles
- o Because of a fear of failure
- o Because we feel guilty for neglecting other things at the same time a project must be completed
- o Because we worry and have a fear of the unknown

o   Because we feel obligated to help someone or a group

o   Because we feel insecure at tackling such a big job

o   Because of a perfectionist syndrome, causing me to worry over needless details

Verne Becker (1981 Today's Christian Woman) suggests that we ask these questions when we are tempted to put something off:

1. What tasks am I putting off?

2. Why don't I want to do this task?

3. How does it affect others and me when I put off that task?

4. How can I break up this project into several smaller tasks?

5. Can I arrange to work alongside a person who has similar responsibilities?

6. Do I tackle the most unpleasant tasks first each day?

7. Have I removed any obstacles that keep me from doing this job?

8. Have I determined the source of any guilt, worry, or fear that may be the root of my procrastination?

9. Can I decide for myself to do this job even though I know I won't like it?

10. Do I congratulate myself each time I avoid procrastinating?

Some time management techniques

o   Set daily goals at the beginning of each day and decide how much time is needed for each task

o   Set a definite deadline for the total task with intermediate targets

o   Develop a habit of scheduling time for high priority tasks each day

o   Find periods of uninterrupted time to complete important work

o   List the tasks you tend to put off, prioritise them and see what can be delegated or dropped

o   Make the most of your best time, that is when you are at your peak and have the most energy

o   Take periodic breaks to clear your mind from completed tasks.

o   Capitalize on unproductive but committed time like driving

o   Say no when things conflict with your own priorities and limitations

o   If you are over committed cut way back

o   Avoid perfectionism. Just show excellence in completing a task and doing it well

"On with it, then, and finish the job! Be as eager to finish it as you were to plan it" (2 Cor. 8:11 TEV).

Reflection

1.   How much does procrastinating affect your ability to lead others?

2.   How are you going to deal with the procrastination tendencies in your life?

3.   Take control of your time - it's a resource you have been given. What habits will you cultivate to improve the use of your time?

Part VII

PRINCIPLES OF STEWARDSHIP

The concept of stewardship is so fundamental to proper Christian leadership that if settled, and put in to practice, it can prevent many mistakes from being made. The biblical perspective on leading is based on service to God and service to others. The prevailing secular perspective is based on control and rulership. A genuine serving leader is predisposed to the concept of stewardship - that the things and people they have the privilege of serving are not made available for selfish motives but for the owner's satisfaction and ambitions. Proper stewardship as a leader will affect many areas. Several of these are included in this section.

64   The Leader as a Steward

Some time back I walked into a facility and came out very sad and disappointed. The once well run facility was now a haven for rats and a monument of how 'state of the art' equipment can quickly go to ruin through neglect. The Director cited lack of finance as the main problem. Regrettably unfinished structures, badly kept roads, broken down walls and poorly maintained buildings are common sites in Africa.

There are few good resources on the important task of maintenance. Clive Douglas of YFC South Africa has produced a very good paper on Property Management and Maintenance. Resources like this are surely needed on our continent. A leader regularly has to deal with legal issues, financial issues, land, buildings, gardens, movable items, vehicles, painting, depreciating items and scores of other similar matters. The framework for considering how to address these demands is the principle of stewardship.

A fresh look at the following Biblical principles on the subject has made me take a critical look at the family, books, clothes, staff and associates, ministry, equipment, knowledge, buildings etc. entrusted to me. There is no doubt I have some work ahead.

1. God owns and retains that ownership of everything and everyone. (Gen. 1:1; 1 Chron 29:14; Luke 14:33; Rom. 11:35-36; Rom. 14:8; Ps. 24:1-2; 50:10-12; Hag. 2:8).

2. God has given man a mandate to be a steward of the earth. To till and keep the land. (Gen. 1:26-27; 2:15). We have a role to play given our ecological crisis.

3. God will judge each of us in respect of our stewardship during our stay here on earth (Luke 19: 12-28; Rom. 14:12).

4. God intends that our stewardship be that of a guardian, curator (Mt. 20:8; Gal. 4:2), a manager or superintendent (Luke 16:2-3; 1 Cor. 4:1-2; Titus 1:7; 1 Pet. 4:10) or that of an executor or dispenser (1Cor. 9:17; Eph. 3:2; Col. 1:25).

5. God entrusts us with different degrees of responsibility (Matt 25:14-15).

6. God desires total dependence on Him for everything (Ps. 104).

7. God expects his stewards to be marked by faithfulness (1 Cor. 4:2).

8. God has the final word and we as stewards need to respond in total obedience to Him as the owner (Ex. 19:5).

9. God wants to bring us in harmony with His value system in order to unlock the 'grace of giving' (Phil 4:14-20; Matt. 6:2-4; Mark 12:41-44; 2 Cor. 8:1-15).

10. God wants us to maintain a balance between generosity and good stewardship (Prov. 6:1-5).

11. God warns us to be clear about our roles. We are stewards and not owners. To assume ownership is thievery (1 Chron. 29:16; Luke 19:13; 1Cor.4: 7).

12. God as the owner sets the standards and expectations for stewardship. It must bring Him pleasure (Matt. 25:14-30). It must be done according to His will before He gives rewards (Luke 19:15-27). It must be proven before trusted to manage more (Luke 12:48). It must be managed assertively for the future (Luke 19:15). It must be guarded (1Tim.6: 20), It is a learned behaviour (1 Tim. 6:17-19; Matt. 28:18-20).

13. God instructs Christians to help each other become better stewards (1 Pet. 4:10).

Reflection

1. Rate on a scale of 1 to 10 your stewardship of what has been entrusted to you by God.

2. What would you have to change or learn in order to be a better steward of what God has entrusted you with?

65 Timeless Wisdom Regarding Finances

It is true that our money is subject to the world's economic systems and I see the effects of it everyday. As Christians we have clear guidelines from Scripture to help us live above the world's system. I have made a personal decision not to be 'crippled' by money problems. It has caused far too many people stress, tension and anxiety. I don't want that. Financial hassles can blur your thinking processes and distort your reasoning ability. It can drain your energy and leaves you emotionally tired.

I have done a thorough study of what the book of Proverbs, the book of wisdom for everyday living, has to say about finances. - There are many wonderful truths that could fill many pages. I have chosen twenty that I think are most relevant for consideration.

1. Give the first part of your income to God before making any financial decisions *(Prov. 3:6, 9-11)*. You can count not only on God's help in your financial life, but also on His bountiful blessings.

2. There are things that are far more valuable than riches. Living wisely usually results in long life, wealth, honour and peace *(Prov. 3:16)*.

3. There needs to be a balance between generosity and stewardship *(Prov. 6:1-5)*.

4. Remember you cannot buy favour with God *(Prov. 11:4)*. He responds to righteousness.

5. To trust in your money will be your folly. Trust in God and you will flourish *(Prov. 11: 28)*.

6. Money brings opportunities and power, but it also has many negative side effects. A full life is better than a life full of money *(Prov. 13:7,8)*.

7. Wealth from gambling quickly disappears but wealth from hard work grows *(Prov. 13:11)*.

8. Do not be gullible just because you are a Christian. Before making a financial decision ask for the relevant facts and check every detail *(Proverbs 14:15; 18:13)*.

9. Money cannot provide safety *(Prov. 18:11)*. It is totally vulnera-

ble against thieves, inflation and corrupt governments. Be God dependent.

10. Watch out - money can tempt us to sacrifice integrity *(Prov. 19:1)*.

11. Take note - when you have money you have many 'friends' *(Prov. 19:4)*. No money, no friends.

12. Be very careful about speculation *(Prov. 21:5)*. Exercise diligence and faithfulness and don't look for quick and easy answers.

13. We need to save for the future *(Prov. 21:20)*. Examine your lifestyle, for God approves foresight and restraint.

14. When you borrow you automatically become a 'slave' of the lender *(Prov. 22:7)*.

15. Good planning in financial management means setting a budget. *(Proverbs 24:3,4)*. Uncontrolled spending causes almost all money woes.

16. Don't burn yourself out making money - it's only temporary. Eternal treasures will never be lost. *(Prov. 23:5)*.

17. Watch your business interests closely *(Prov. 27:24)*.

18. Keep away from get-rich-quick schemes *(Proverbs 28:20)*.

19. Whether you have over enough or barely enough to live on, both can lead to problems *(Proverbs 30:8,9)*. Watch your attitude regarding money.

20. Do not borrow if you have no intention of repayment *(Prov. 37:21)*.

Reflection

1. In which areas of your financial stewardship do you want to become more effective?

2. Which principles do you find hardest to implement and how will you overcome the challenges they present to you?

66   Ethics in the Workplace

A year ago I bought myself a bag to make it difficult for customs officials to find my laptop. But I soon realised that I was misrepresenting myself. When we talk about ethics we concern ourselves about
the judgement of what is right or wrong. Ethics reflect one's character and values. It is about adhering to rules, codes of conduct and
making correct choices. It is deciding on what ought to be instead
of what is.

> *"Always tell the truth and you never have to remember what you
> said"*
>
> *- A.L. Osborn*

Too often personal-gain, greed, self-interest and achieving maximum advantage over others are the main reasons for unethical
decisions.

Ethics must permeate every aspect of our lives. We need ethics in
relationships, in the exercise of authority, in our communications, in
our travel arrangements, in the exercise of leadership and in our
personal and business dealings.

In a Kairos International manual, 'Leadership beyond Management'
it says it so much better. "To try and justify unethical decisions is
nothing short of self-deception. The problem at the end of the day
is that we stand the risk of actually believing a lie. Truth and reality
become clouded...reality must be truth and truth must be reality.
When perceptions are seen as reality, the truth is clouded."

We misrepresent ourselves when...

o   We do all the right things but with wrong motives

o   We give generously so we can manipulate groups, policies and
    decisions

o   We blame others for our shortcomings

o   We exploit people for our own gain

o   We use other people's work and pretend it is our own

o   We make promises that we know we cannot deliver

o   We speak negatively about others to promote ourselves

o   We fail to return calls or instruct others to lie on our behalf because we cannot face people.

o   We cheat and doctor our reports in order to look good

o   We use others or manipulate the system to climb the corporate ladder…the list goes on and on

The leader is responsible to ensure a high standard with it comes to ethics in the workplace. This requires that the leader:

1.   Create an ethical culture - It will attract the best workers

2.   Ensure their ethics are consistent - let it reflect your values

3.   Make ethical choices - even when there is an element of risk associated

4.   Have a concern for the common good - practice good ethics

Raymond L. Hilgert, Philip H. Lochhaas, James L. Truesdell in their book 'Christian Ethics in the Workplace' give us some applied tests for ethical decision-making:

1.   Am I operating within the limits of the law?

2.   How would the broader public react to my decision?

3.   What are the long-term consequences of my decision?

4.   Are my motives pure and for the benefit of others and the organisation?

5.   Do I have a clear conscious about my decision?

To be ethical could mean:

1.   Paying a price for being honest

2.   Going out of my way to keep my word

3.   Taking an unpopular position

4.   Admitting my mistakes

5.   Doing what is best for the group and not just myself

As a friend of mine once pointed out -

o   Unethical business practices could lead to your ultimate demise

o   Ethics could determine the success or failure of the next generation

o Ethics is a never-ending pursuit especially with new technological discoveries like genetic engineering.

o Your ethics will determine your reputation and you cannot place a monetary value on reputation

Reflection

1. What are your views on ethics? Name some of the ethical dilemmas you face, and how do you deal with them?

2. In which ways does your organisation violate ethical principles, and what are you going to do to change that?

67 Principles Relating to Politics

As Christian, our role in society is one that we must be faithful to play. The challenge is that there are a few different perspective on this topic. As leaders of Christian organizations or ministries we may find ourselves in a bit of a dilemma. When it comes to politics, it's almost impossible to take some community action without being unfairly labelled by one side or the other.

Members of my team have asked me my thoughts on the Christian's involvement in politics. No one can give a comprehensive answer on one page but I submit the following principles for consideration which have helped my perspective on the subject.

1. **The quality of a Christian's life is not determined by a government system.** There are many repressive systems around the world, which are unable to dampen the zeal and commitment of Christians who live under them. Don't rely on the state for spiritual direction and answers.

2. **Christians throughout history have had different perspectives on the role of the Christian in politics.** Some are 'world denying' and emphasise the fact the real kingdom for the Christian is heaven. Others are 'world affirming' and maintain that since the world is God's world we ought to be involved in it through politics and social action. For me both are necessary if we are going to be faithful to the Scripture.

3. **The church and the state differ fundamentally from each other.** The state cannot exist without the exercise of force. It is sectional in its dealings and concerned about its own survival. The church reflects the Kingdom of God. It exercises faith, hope and love and is all inclusive.

4. **Sin is universal and all people are sinners.** So be careful of selective depravity and implying that one group is more depraved or corrupt than another. Depravity and moral corruption are universal and no one group has a monopoly on sin. Realise that you cannot bring about real change in your own strength. We need to mobilise God's people to pray for our nations.

5. **For the Christian the Cross implies the value of each individual, despite the fact that we are all sinners.** Not all

people are God's children but all people are made in God's image. Individuals ought to be treated by government as having value irrespective of tribal, social and religious status.

6. **A leader must have the favour and support of the majority of the people he or she wants to lead.** If you are appointed then you must persuade your followers that you are worthy to lead. If you are elected then you must concentrate on those who did not elect you. If you have appointed yourself then you have to win people over to share your convictions. If you have been born into the position then your task is more difficult.

7. **The Cross has another implication.** Reconciliation between God and man but also between man and man. Our desire should be reconciliation and not violent confrontation. We do not resort to violence but we must speak out when we see injustice. We can and should apply non-violent pressure to change evil practices. We must tell political leaders what we think of certain policies. Our opinions matter and they must be voiced. Everything must be done in love and that doesn't necessarily mean being weak and silent.

8. **All members of parliament are trustees of God's power and should use it to foster an orderly society** and not one which is in chaos (Romans 13). So then as Christians we ought to aim for an orderly society (Jeremiah 9:23-24).

9. **There is no such thing as a 'Christian State'.** The church does not exist to serve the state. It is not the church's role to fulfil nationalistic aspirations. Theology must not be displaced by ideology. The church is an alternative community serving the causes of the Kingdom and ensuring that we have good governance. She must be salt and light in communities. Christians have a crucial role to play by making sure that there is a high degree of justice and integrity. We need to do all we can to restrain selfish politicians and promote servant leaders who seek the welfare of others. We are not obsessed with party politics but are concerned about the moral base a country needs to survive.

10. **The doctrine of the return of Christ also has implications.** This means while we are striving for change in society we must

remember that the final and complete solution will only come when Christ returns and sets up His kingdom and abolishes all earthly governments.

Reflection

1. As a leader, how does this compare with what is happening today?

2. Which of your political views do you find hardest to reconcile with Scriptural principles?

67 Respecting the Work of Others

The emerging electronic technologies have raised important issues of copyright and ethics regarding the intellectual and creative 'property' of others. Pirating is defined as 'illegal copying or broadcasting without a license, illegal use or reproduction of printed or recorded material which is protected by copyright'. In Africa 'pirating' is almost a way of life.

As a musician and novice producer I have faced this problem personally. Our first music cassette in Madagascar was pirated and sold widely across the island. We were required to pay a large fee to secure copyright, which is just a scam. I have seen the shelves of radio stations stacked with illegal copies of music materials. Recently I had a run in with a fellow Christian worker who copies and distributes hundreds of other people's cassettes in the name of 'evangelism'. His argument, 'The end justifies the means' and the laws of the world do not apply to him. Whether it is a cassette, CD, video, DVD or book there is just no regard by many for copyright.

Apparently musicians in Madagascar are fighting a losing battle. They even went so far as to write a song on the subject but that even failed. One of my staff believes that it is easier to fight AIDS than the copyright battle. In South Africa we have seen YFC materials printed by churches as their own.

Interestingly enough, Christians are as guilty of this as non Christians. We 'steal' training materials, sermons, quotes, ideas, hymns and songs without acknowledging anyone. Christians need to demonstrate Biblical values and superior standards in this regard.

1. There must be a high regard for the work of others

This implies that you are showing admiration and consideration for the achievements and hard work of others. In 1 Peter 2:17 it says, "Show proper respect to everyone..." As Christians we need to give recognition to each other and hold each other in high esteem. In 1 Corinthians 16:18 the Apostle Paul encourages the church to give recognition to those who 'refreshed him in the spirit'. Giving recognition to others is usually an incentive and a great motivation to do even better.

2. There must be a high level of integrity regarding the work of others

I read sometime back of a preacher (can't find the article and do not remember his name) who tells of how he visited a church and heard one of his own sermons being preached verbatim. One of the Ten Commandments we like to quote to children is, "Thou shalt not steal". If Moses were alive today, I bet he would have included 'copyrighted materials' in his list of what stealing entails (Lev. 6:1-7).

3. There must be a high standard of excellence maintained in the work of others.

It is embarrassing, to say the least, how other people's materials lose their quality, worth and effectiveness when they are repeatedly copied, when they are constantly being downgraded and cheapened. In the Living Bible we read in Philippians 4:8 "…and dwell on the fine, good things in others…" The NIV says, "whatever is admirable - if anything is excellent or praise worthy - think about such things." 2 Corinthians 8:7 implies excellence in all things. I have personally confronted some radio stations regarding their violations and periodically give them gifts of original materials, so they can have an appreciation for quality. At a local Bible school, I even had a debate on the issue of students photocopying entire books.

4. There must be a high regard for the law, which protects the work of others

The copyright laws protect artists, inventors, writers, producers and manufacturers. Today people are being prosecuted for breaking this law. According to Romans 13 we rebel against what God has instituted if we rebel against the authorities. Our freedom in Christ does not mean we have a license to do what we want - read Galatians 5. In fact this freedom will cause us to serve each other and what better way than to protect the work of others.

5. There must be a high disregard for the excuses when the work of others is violated

A common reason given by many who break the copyright law is a monetary one. Maybe the reason why we never have enough money to buy is because; over the years we have habitually stolen from others. We think it is okay to break the law in order to have things or to do God's work. God responds to righteousness and will make a way for us to have what we need. The Scripture says that He will supply our needs according to his riches in glory (Phil 4:19).

Reflection

1. How much pirated material do you have in your possession?

2. What is your response going to be?

3. What is the most effective way you can ensure that the work of others is respected in your organisation and circles of influence?

69 Maintenance

In the past I have had several passionate discussions around the subject of maintenance. In my present town it is a major concern for the new local authority. Its widespread neglect on the African continent is an undisputed fact. Corruption and poor leadership has made many parts of this region an ecological disaster. Added to this are the neglect of vehicles, machinery, technological apparatus and equipment of every kind.

This is not an easy subject to deal with because of real cultural, political, educational and economic factors. For example:

1. In some cultures a house is built to crawl in at night while in others they are homes to live in at all times.

2. In the new South Africa, I remember whites complaining about the neglect of hospitals, while blacks were just too happy to at last have access to one.

3. In Madagascar poverty is a real thing. People have daily survival on their minds and maintenance is a distant priority.

4. In Africa, colonials must take a measure of blame for the lack of ownership, poor stewardship, corruption, ignorance and poor leadership that is prevalent today. They literally made maintenance a foreign concept.

5. In others, we see those who are just tardy, lazy, negligent and undisciplined.

There are a number of reasons why we need to talk about maintenance.

1. Anything that is maintained has a prolonged life

2. Anything that is maintained saves costs

3. Anything that is maintained may increase in worth

4. Anything that is maintained can bring you much joy

5. Anything that is maintained can bring you favour with others

There are also a number of Biblical principles on stewardship to support this area of maintenance

o   God own and retains ownership of everything and everyone we have

o   God has given us a mandate to look after everything and everyone he has entrusted to us o   God will judge us in respect of our stewardship during our stay here on earth

o   God intends that our stewardship be that of a guardian, curator, manager, superintendent, executor or dispenser.

o   God expects his stewards to be marked by faithfulness

o   God, as the owner, sets the standards and expectations for stewardship

Some practical considerations

1.   Define and establish clear maintenance standards - refer to the world's best practices

2.   Allow for maintenance and preventative maintenance in the budget

3.   Implement a clear maintenance strategy with accountability

4.   Use creativity to develop a culture of maintenance in every part of your operation

5.   Involve change agents who can drive an incremented approach to maintenance

6.   Take heed of maintenance standards and directions that come with equipment, machinery, vehicles etc.

7.   Set an example by starting today (start in your home)

But please note, this is just not about property and things but about maintaining relationships. It can save marriages, produce healthy families, keep staff turnover low and prolong friendships.

Reflection

1.   How do you currently deal with maintenance issues? Do you wait for things to break first?

2.   In which areas of your life will maintenance make a huge difference? (Not material things only).

3.   Now that you have a different perspective on maintenance, design a programme of maintenance for as many areas in your life as possible. Share those with your team for their feedback.

Part VIII

TEAM EFFECTIVENESS

Successful organizations function differently than a group of people simply working together. Successful organzations are characterized by teamwork and team spirit. The first of these, teamwork is the most important. Too often leaders try to take a shortcut but focussing on the hype of team spirit. Without a fundamental commitment to working as a team, team spirit is pretty hollow. To achieve high performance results it is becoming increasingly clear that a high performance team is needed. Team building is an important responsibility for a leader. The leader is responsible to clarify the vision, align the members and define the unique contributions and roles for each. Then they must carefully manage the resulting interdependency well. It's pretty basic stuff but not very easy to do. This section looks at the important area of creating team effectiveness.

70 Building Community

There is nothing more complimentary for a leader to hear than to have an outsider describe your team as a community. Many workers spend nearly half the time that they are awake at work. They work and interact with colleagues and supervisors. Like any group of individuals together for an extended period of time the quality of the relationships formed will make all the difference in the world. The challenge therefore to leaders is to transform their organisation into a community where their people have roots, can feel a sense of belonging and identity, show appreciation for each other and know that they matter to those around them. Where they can achieve far more than if they were alone and where shared values are embraced.

"We consider it normal to seek community and abnormal to shy away from it" James Lea Beall. He goes on to describe basic values for the establishment and building of community:

o   Meeting basic human needs - the ability of the community to supply every kind of need

o   Satisfying the need to belong - becoming a member or part of a community is an important aspect

o   Fulfilling the need for significance - the community making us feel special in some way

o   Facilitating the need for approval - the need for commendation and praise in the community

Community as defined by Evelyn Eaton Whitehead and James D. Whitehead is "a gathering of people who support one another's performance...community is the place where we learn to hold one another".

"I am of the persuasion if we could create an awareness of community in the workplace, more leaders would emerge." Scott Peck

John W. Gardner suggests that "What we think of as a failure of leadership on the contemporary scene may be traceable to a breakdown in the sense of community...leaders are community builders" He also concludes that the building of community "is one of the highest and most essential skills a leader can command" and suggests the following ingredients of genuine community:

o   Wholeness incorporating diversity

o   A shared culture

o   Good internal communication

o   Caring, trust and teamwork

o   Group maintenance and government

o   Participation and the sharing of leadership tasks

o   Developing of young people

o   Links with the outside world

John M. Perkins in his book 'Beyond Charity' describes what should happen in an authentic local church community.

o   Pain is absorbed (Luke 4; Matt 11:28)

o   Hope is proclaimed

o   God is proclaimed as the sovereign authority (Matt 28:18-19)

o   People are brought together (Mark 11:17)

o   The needy benefit (Acts 4:34-35)

o   God's character is reflected

o   The vulnerable are protected (Isaiah 58:1,6)

In Acts 2:43-45 a community is described. They had no church building but they came together, had all things in common, sold their property and possessions and shared them with those who had need. As leaders, we need to give ourselves to the important task of community building.

Reflection

1. Observe your people - their behaviour and comments. To what extent have you built a sense of community in your organisation, and how will you improve that?

2. To what extent do your own insecurities prevent you from building community, and what are you going to do to overcome those insecurities or work around them?

71 Leading a Small Group

My first exposure to small group dynamics was in the mid-seventies when a university student placed a document in my hand describing small group ministry. By that time I had only known leaders preaching to large groups and monologue discussions, if you can call it discussions. This small group concept was revolutionary to me.

Now the importance of small groups is well known and many churches are making good use of the benefits of this type of ministry. In the broader world more businesses, educational institutions, community organizations and others are making the most of what happens when small groups (teams, focus groups, task forces etc.) get together.

Here are some principles related to small group ministry that may help your leadership in this area:

Establish and monitor for enhancement the following in the experience of the small groups:

- *Dialogue*
- *Sense of belonging*
- *Development of spiritual gifts, talent and personality*
- *Affirmation*
- *Experimentation*
- *Adoption of new methods*
- *Simplicity*
- *Atmosphere of trust and care*
- *Bible discussed in simple language*
- *Truth shared rather than taught*
- *Friendships developed*
- *The Word translated into everyday experience*
- *Accountability*
- *Sense of achievement*
- *Recognition of accomplishment*

● *The ideal size, 8-13 members*

Leadership is critical for small groups to be successful. Make sure you are prepared to adequately train the leaders you need. They will make or break the program. Potential leaders should manifest the following emotional qualities:

1. Mature and not oversensitive to criticism

2. Do not feel threatened by difficult questions

3. Teachable and acknowledges that he/she does not know all the answers

4. Humble spirit

5. Transparent and vulnerable

6. Has hunger for Word and good Bible knowledge

7. Not a novice

8. Good sense of humour but not at the expense of others

9. Should have ongoing development and should broaden own horizons

Small group leaders need the following skills to be developed in order to provide effective leadership:

1. Get people involved (maximum participation)

2. Make dialogue the emphasis

3. Be enthusiastic

4. Learn how to motivate

5. Learn communication skills

6. Allow time to think before answering

7. Team development

8. Keep each person accountable

9. Keep records

10. Good follow through

11. Allow for optimum expression

12. Advance preparation

13. Good start and ending

14. Keep the discussion orderly and on track

15. Maintain control

16. Set the tone for the quality and depth of the discussions

17. Pre-meeting arrangements allow for intimacy

Reflection

1. Rate yourself on a scale of 1 to 10 in each of the 9 emotional requirements mentioned above.

2. What feedback would inform you that you are effective in the leadership techniques mentioned above?

3. Of the 18 characteristics of small groups, what is most difficult and what is easiest for you to implement?

72 Building Unity in Your Team

Recently I walked into a situation and could virtually smell the divide in the group. Unfortunately disunity is found everywhere in society - in businesses, families, neighbourhoods, schools, governments and churches. Disunity usually breeds rebellion, power struggles and intolerance. Some leaders refuse to acknowledge that there is a problem of disunity in their team. Others have the inability to do something about it.

In the broader sense disunity is often caused by some obvious factors:

o   Socio-economic barriers

o   Educational, class and opportunity disparities

o   Political, ideological and religious strife

o   Racial, cultural and tribal conflict

But, these differences need not be a source of disunity. We benefit by looking a little deeper at the issue. According to John Stott in his book 'Issues facing Christians today' he suggests that 'we cannot abolish all inequalities but the inequality of the privilege we should seek to abolish.' Any difference, which is accompanied by an inherent privilege regardless of merit, creates the tensions that can flame into division.

There may be other reasons for disunity in a working team context:

o   Some are just not team players

o   Some lack commitment to the leader

o   Some seek pre-eminence

o   Some assert their own agendas

o   Some try to assert control

o   Some have inability to walk in agreement

o   Some have an independent spirit

o   Some are intolerable of others

o   Some breed an unhealthy spirit of competition

o   Some just cannot maintain friendships

o   Some are on a mission to promote themselves

o   Some are in the status trap and driven by prestige

o   Some are just plainly self-centred

o   Some are threatened by the success of others

o   Some have an inability to serve

o   Some just have a critical spirit

THINGS TO NOTE.

A couple of common misunderstandings when it comes to team unity:

- In unity there's diversity and harmony. Not uniformity and unison, where everyone looks, dresses and acts alike. People have a right to be different and a right to disagree but one should not be disagreeable and divisive.

- In unity there is not necessarily the absence of conflict - conflict is like 'the sandpaper of life'. There is a positive side to conflict that can bring out the beauty and the best in a team. Conflict must be managed and the sooner the better.

The following key pointers will encourage unity:

1. The importance of dialogue. Good internal communication is vital. Always seek ways to encourage all to participate.

2. The importance of servant leadership. Someone with a servant spirit is not threatened by the success of another.

3. The importance of building team. That is, participation and sharing of tasks and regular evaluation of progress made.

4. The importance of community. Where everyone is encouraged, supported, respected and where there is a common purpose, sense of achievement, belonging and togetherness.

5. The importance of ensuring group maintenance and good governance.

Jesus in John 17:21-23 prays to the Father for His disciples to be one. The apostle Paul sets forth some principles in Philippians 2: 1-7 for preserving unity.

Reflection

1. Rate the level of unity in your team. What are some of the gaps in unity within your team?

2. How will you use your newfound knowledge to foster unity within your team?

73 Building Team Spirit

How do successful sports teams build team spirit in the midst of so much competition? I recently witnessed South Africa beating the West Indies in the fifth and final match of a one-day cricket series. On more than one occasion I heard members of the winning team refer to the team effort and team spirit.

On the same night the South African soccer team, Bafana Bafana was eliminated in the first round of the African Cup of Nations with the team morale at an all time low. In fact many predicted that this would be the case and one commentator even suggested that what happened on the field was just a reflection of events off the field.

In Genesis 2:18-25; 11:1-9 we have descriptions of teamwork. They are characterised by understanding, one language, common speech, agreement, and common direction, shared goals and planned action. Through these the Lord indicates the attributes of teamwork that will bring about breakthroughs and victories.

How do you build a team? Here is a long list that reflects what I think it takes to accomplish this task:

- o   Define the kind of members you need
- o   Establish clear criteria for team selection
- o   Look for team chemistry (a relational fit)
- o   Build cohesiveness, trust and care
- o   Enjoy special moments together
- o   Focus team efforts towards a unified goal
- o   Establish role clarity for each member
- o   Bring them together to complement each other
- o   Demonstrate appreciation for each other's strengths
- o   Give ownership
- o   Use team-building exercises
- o   Reward the team for work well done
- o   Negotiate and work through conflicting goals and priorities
- o   Operate within boundaries of principles and core values
- o   Ensure understanding of the leader's role

o Facilitate effective team processes

o Hold each member accountable

o Encourage clear, honest and open communication

o Resolve interpersonal conflicts effectively and quickly

o Ensure effectiveness of high quality decisions

o Measure progress made

o Invite feedback on team performances

o Encourage servant attitudes

o Set them free to become what God intended them to be

o Affirm team members

o Share experiences

o instill a sense of belonging

o Ensure development of each member

o Protect those that are vulnerable

o Help individuals take responsibility for their lives

o Treat all members as equal

o Encourage collaboration

o Move away from individual victories to team victories

o Provide conditions for empowerment

o Remember no two persons are alike (different things motivate different people)

o Encourage loyalty and commitment

o Model and encourage transparency

Reflection

1. What is your understanding of the difference between unity in a team and team spirit?

2. What are some of the practical ways in which you will implement the ideas listed above in order to improve the spirit in your team?

74 Communicating Your Message

The development of quality team relationships depends quite a bit on the quality of communication on the part of the leader. After listening to a weekend of speeches and evaluating its effectiveness with a group of students, I came to the definite conclusion that many speakers are more interested in speech making than communicating. Many are so caught up with their content that they lose their audience.

Do we really care whether people will listen long enough to hear what we have to say? As Christian leaders we have the awesome responsibility of communicating spiritual truth and we must evaluate constantly our effectiveness if we are to impact this present generation with the demands of Christ. As we prepare to communicate, particularly through public address, let's consider the following:

- ### Make it imaginative

    In Scripture we see Jesus appealing to the senses and imagination of the locals. This He did by storytelling. Today we are still referring to His many profound parables. Let's find stories whether from Scripture, everyday life or from our own experiences that embody the truths we want to get across. Listeners must feel they are participating in the narratives being told.

- ### Make it answer questions

    Someone said "great teachers get people to discover truth for themselves". Question-asking moves people from being spectators to being participators. Develop the art of asking rhetorical questions. They may not answer you directly but it will encourage them to answer questions that will lead them to the truth.

- ### Make it personal

    People would rather listen to real experiences than an eloquent speech. Today's young people can tell if the truth is real to you or not. Let's be transparent and talk about our struggles, experiences and victories as they relates to the topic we are sharing.

- ## Make it transformational

  It should inspire people to action. It should be more than just information-giving but mobilise people to ask the question 'what next' or 'how can I make a difference' or 'what is my responsibility'.

- ## Make it relevant

  Relate what people do not know to what they do know. Relate to everyday issues, like school, studies, home, friendships, sport, music, unemployment, poverty etc. Relate to people's needs, pain, interests and lifestyles. Jesus was a good example and demonstrated this as He used everyday issues like sheep, bread, light etc as a bridge to convey His message.

- ## Make it coherent

  The stories, questions, thoughts, points, disclosures must be held together by a strong central theme. Whether your talk is cyclic or follows a systematic point form make sure that it holds together with this central theme. Avoid trying to cover every imaginable subject in one talk.

- ## Make it dynamic

  Your talk should have variations in loudness, expression and appropriate gestures, not forgetting good eye contact. It should be forceful and should produce enough changes and action for effects. Too often a monotone voice can put an audience to sleep.

- ## Make it Biblical

  We must instill a hunger for the Word of God. We must show the relevance of Scripture to the issues of today. We must bring to life the Biblical characters and stories in a way that will relate to today's generation. We must communicate the central theme of Scripture, which is the salvation of mankind and give people the opportunity to receive Christ and experience the truth of the Word.

Reflection

1. What would you most like to change in order to improve your effectiveness as a communicator?

2. Ask three people to rate your next public speaking engagement in terms of the points mentioned above.

75 Screening and Selecting Potential Workers

As part of becoming an increasingly dynamic and growing ministry we have learnt a valuable lesson. History has taught us to make screening and selection a higher priority. Failure to screen a person's past, thoroughly, is 'looking for trouble'.

Geoff Rutter gives this important principle ignored by many leaders. "The past behaviour is the most reliable (though not perfect) way of predicting future behaviour".

A critical self-analysis of my own failures in this regard in 30 years of Christian ministry shows that I ignored important principles taught to me by my predecessors. Its one thing to agree with the importance of careful selection of staff and volunteers, but another to put it into action.

A healthy screening policy:

- Confirms that information on application forms is correct
- Determines the maturity level of a candidate
- Certifies the candidate's financial history
- Exposes commitment levels
- Establishes compatibility with other team members
- Enlightens you to the level of experience, skill and training
- Draws attention to any physical or health limitations
- Ensures correct placements
- Ascertains the level of competency
- Verifies the leadership style
- Creates a safe environment
- Prevents unnecessary lawsuits

Paul Chaffee in his book, 'Accountable Leadership' states, "Screening may sound dismaying, particularly when long-time members are involved. The tragedy of abuse by an employer or volunteer is infinitely more dismaying"

Geoff Rutter outlines common mistakes in interviewing and selection of personnel:

1. Asking questions requiring "yes" or "no" could result in faked answers for the sake of impression

2. Asking theoretical questions results in theoretical answers

3. Allowing one outstanding characteristic to influence you unduly and obscure your objectivity

4. Allowing vague, theoretical, future-orientated statements and opinions, instead of facts and past examples.

5. Disclosing what you are testing or helping them give the answers

6. Equating experience with competence

7. Equating spirituality with ability

8. Allowing misinterpretation of Phil. 4:13, which has nothing to do with skill and ability

9. Being manipulated by the "God has called me" statement.

10. Being deceived by physical appearance

11. Weak spouse support

12. Assuming that training can correct skill deficiencies

13. Deadline pressure

14. Candidate is a friend of a high-up person or has contacts

Lee Iacocca states, "I've seen too many cases where somebody was in the wrong job for years. More often than not, there was no way for management to find that out until it was too late."

Consider the following criteria for selecting people

1. Faithfulness

2. Giftedness

3. Training and skill

4. Credibility

5. Job history

The Apostle Paul selected Timothy as his assistant because "All the believers in Lystra and Iconium spoke well of Timothy" (Acts 16:2).

Reflection

1. What mistakes have you made screening and selecting staff? What will you have to do to avoid repeating them?

2. How will you go about establishing an effective system of selecting staff, using the criteria for selecting people outlined above?

76 Creating a Job Description

One of the critical areas in developing a high performing team is role clarity. At the most pragmatic level this involves clearly describing particular contributions, or jobs. I have been made fully aware of frustrations over lack of clarity from staff regarding their job. Unfortunately some jobs involve role conflict, role ambiguity and work overload or underload.

- Some work without a job description.

- Some never look at their job description

- Some are evaluated without having a job description

- Some try to control their work without a job description

- Some misuse their job descriptions to avoid doing certain work

- Some job descriptions do not accurately reflect what people are doing

- Some have a job description that has never been discussed with them

There is a biblical basis for a job description

●	Exodus 3:1-12	Job description given to Moses
●	Genesis 37: 5-11	Job description given to Joseph
●	Genesis 12: 1-3	Job description given to Abraham
●	Matthew 28:19-20	Job description given to disciples
●	Acts 26: 16-19	Job description given to Paul

Definition: A job description is a written instrument that portrays in a systematic, concise, and logical fashion what is expected of an individual who fills a certain position - Robert Welch

It should answer the following questions

1. What is my title and location of work? To designate and identify the job with a realistic title

2. What is my principal function or purpose? A quick explanation of what the job is supposed to accomplish

3. How do I fit into the organisation? To locate my job in the organisation

4. What makes me qualified for the position? Spells out the education and experience I have to perform the job

5. What are my responsibilities? Comprehensive list of what must be done and output expected

6. What authority do I have? How much decision making power I have

7. Who looks to me for direction? What staff will I be responsible for

8. Who do I look to for direction? To whom am I responsible

9. Who do I work with closely? The people I daily relate to

10. What special conditions and extra work is expected? Unusual features required like long hours, driving etc

The fundamentals of a job description involve the following:

o Should be viewed as a formal agreement

o Should state what standards you expect

o Should be dynamic and allow for changes when necessary

o Should take into consideration whether people are full time, part time or volunteers

o Should be agreed on by the person reporting to you

o Should be drawn up by the person (if already in the organisation) and then discussed

o Should be given to a new person coming into the organisation

o Should have a date and be reviewed annually - it gets obsolete quickly

o Should have a purpose which gives a concise summary of the job

o Should have scope which gives parameters of the job

o Should have specific responsibility with equal authority

o Should be viewed with maturity and allow for innovation and creativity

The three essential qualities of a job description

- Responsibility
- Authority
- Accountability

Reflection

1. How clearly do the people you lead understand their job description, and how well do you communicate job descriptions?

2. If you had to improve on your ability to draw up job descriptions with the people you lead, what areas would you concentrate on improving?

77 Dealing with Late-Coming

One of the greatest ways we can demonstrate our respect for others is by honouring their time. Too often we become victims of some-one else's time management dilemma? This bad habit is a particu-lar problem when practiced by leaders. Some leaders are plagued by habits that are ingrained and hard to break. One such habit is a lack of punctuality. Some of our lives are so chaotic that we end up wasting other people's valuable time and hard earned money.

Late-comers are people who:

- Do not have a manageable way of organising their time
- Are just undisciplined, lazy and often come from a family of late-comers
- Can never get work done and have all kinds of things to do at the last minute
- Think they can always do better
- Resent being reminded about their problem
- Usually have charming personalities with a bag full of excuses
- Are unable to say 'no' to themselves and other people
- Do too many things at the same time and have difficulty com-pleting anything
- Respond too all kinds of emergencies
- Take on too much and discover that time is a problem
- Are just poor at planning, prioritising and scheduling their com-mitments
- Allow all kinds of emergencies to interrupt their schedule
- Have an inability to pace themselves and plan for the unexpect-ed

"Spend a day taking note of how many times you are affected by someone else's lack of planning" - Patty Marler

When working in close collaboration with others on a team there are a number of unfortunate consequences:

1. The constant need to look for excuses for being late

2. Not being able to get through the agenda in the time allocated

3. The strain it places on relationships with associates who are irritated and discouraged

4. The resentment it creates with others who are always early

5. The negative and domino effect it has on later appointments

Here are some suggestions on how to deal with the problem of punctuality:

o Face the facts and stop living in denial. Admit you have a problem and that change is needed

o Think about the negative impact it has on your effectiveness as a leader

o Analyse your time patterns and make some honest self-observations

o Take responsibility for your actions and make needed changes - get help and be accountable to someone for your time

o Start to modify your behaviour by continuous effort that will result in continuous growth, maturity, wisdom, integrity and accountability

o Use evaluation to grow from experience

o Clarify your values and make a personal commitment to be on time

"All things are difficult before they are easy" - Thomas Fuller; "Work hard at whatever you do" (Ecclesiastes 9:10).

Reflection

1. What are some of the common excuses you have for being late?

2. In which ways are you affected by other people's lack of planning, and in which ways do you affect others by your own lack of planning?

78 Evaluating Your Team

It has been said that you treasure what you measure. If, as a leader, you value team performance and then you need to systematically find a means to measure how your team is doing in key areas.

The following is an example of a simple assessment tool. Assess today how well your team is doing by considering the following characteristics. It should help you determine their performance and how well you have built up your team. Give them a rating 0 (low) to 10 (high). It is also important for your as a leader to obtain value feedback from the team members on their perceptions and experience. The same survey can be filled out by team members. Doing this should provide some good material for an open team discussion on how to improve performance.

1. We know what we are supposed to accomplish and are committed to those goals.

2. We effectively negotiate and work through conflicting goals and priorities.

3. We have role clarity with the right people doing the right jobs with nothing left undone.

4. We are interdependent to a large degree in most areas. We know we need each other to accomplish goals.

5. We are clear about the role of the leader.

6. We have effective facilitation of key team processes, and effective team membership.

7. We experience trust, respect for strengths, acceptance of differences and diversities and understanding of goals, interests and weaknesses of each other.

8. We have open, clear, honest communication. We share relevant, quick and accurate communication with each other and hear each other's opinions. We resolve interpersonal conflicts effectively.

9. We have an effective, systematic method of making high quality decisions and we are good at executing our strategies and action plans.

10. Our meetings are efficient and characterised by effective communication.

11. We measure our progress and receive prompt, reliable, useful feedback on our performances.

Reflection

1. What weaknesses and strengths do the scores highlight, and what does that suggest in terms of the needs within your team?

2. What would you have to change in order to develop a dynamic, effective team?

79   Getting Your People to Deliver

Recently I've been to a meeting where a group discovered a strategic document that took ages to prepare but was filed away and forgotten. Often we make plans but fail to deliver. The ability to get things done can be the difference between success and failure. Board, staff and committee meetings must be more than just talk shops.

In Africa we are good at talking about and analysing problems but to act is often another story. We have become professional analysts and masters at talking about talking. Too many of our leaders have become great orators with very little to show. We make unrealistic promises to appease shareholders or followers but have no idea how to get our people to deliver on those promises. We need leaders who have the ability to make things happen.

The next time you have the opportunity to travel through our continent take note of the many unfinished structures. We start but often do not complete what we have set out to do.

Over the years I have had to learn principles, techniques and disciplines to help my teams produce results.

1. **It starts with the leader who must be a model executer.** A leader must be more than just a talker but results-driven. It is therefore important for leaders to put in place those management structures that will facilitate the execution of their plans.

2. **Be purpose and vision directed.** Too often we are sidetracked. A buzz of activities and programmes does not mean you are achieving anything. Turn vision into strategies that can be filtered down to the frontline people who must implement them.

3. **Display goals and objectives where people can be reminded about priorities and reflect on their performance.** Success must be measured against goals. Be obsessed with outcomes. Deadlines and targets must be honoured. Keep people accountable for specific results.

4. **Action plans must become part of our culture.** Our days must start with action notes. Action minutes should become the norm. Long discussions must conclude with concrete actions. Minutes of meetings must be reviewed, analysed and followed

through to see if action steps were fulfilled.

5. **Empower people so that they can make the most of their time.** People need role clarity, leadership, skills and tools to get things done. People are the core means by which we implement. Often we spend millions on the infrastructure but have no people development plan. I know of companies who have state of the art equipment but no one with the skill to operate them.

6. **Develop assessment tools to measure performance.** Performance management and accountability will ensure productivity. Make it a habit to give people immediate and frequent feedback on their performance.

7. **Create ownership and an environment where people can pursue a course of action.** Develop a culture of entrepreneurialism and creativity where new ideas are nurtured and change encouraged.

8. **Engage your folk in collaborative ways that will energise them to play a major role in your organisation's mission and get them out of their comfort zones.** People need to be given challenging jobs where they can take certain risks.

9. **In our succession planning we must understand the roles needed to get people to produce.** There are differences between technical roles and management/leadership roles. People with technical ability do not necessarily have the skills to get teams to perform and produce. To get teams to produce you need a leader who motivates, encourages, builds confidence and gives direction.

Throughout scripture this principle is reinforced.

o   God finished the work He started. In **Genesis 2:1** we read "The heavens and the earth were completed in their entire vast array". He shows us the importance of being result orientated.

o   Talk without action could lead to poverty. "All hard work brings a profit but mere talk only leads to poverty" **Proverbs 14:23**

o   On the cross Jesus uttered "It is finished". He had accomplished what he came to do. To bring salvation to mankind by his works, teachings and life.

o   Paul could confidently say, "I have run the race".

o   God wants us to be productive and to show fruit for our labours. In **Luke 19:12-23** everything was taken away from an unproductive steward.

o   Productivity in small ways may lead to greater opportunities to produce. **Matt 25:21** "Be faithful with a few things and you will be in charge of many things".

"It has long since come to my attention that people of accomplishment rarely sat back and let things happen to them. They went out and happened to things" - Elinor Smith

---

Reflection

1.   Think of something you want to accomplish in the future. What does the end product look like, and do you know how to plan to get there in bite sized chunks?

2.   Rate your own delivery ability. To what extent have you created an environment within which delivery / finishing can take place?

80 Keeping your Team Motivated

One of our challenges as leaders is to keep the members of our team motivated. During a time of political turmoil in Madagascar there were many challenging distractions. In our town businesses were discouraged, people lost their jobs and fuel was scarce. For weeks school kids walked around aimlessly. Foreigners left the country. People became demotivated as they waited for the next political move. Trying to inspire and motivate others in this kind of situation is hard. A good leader is continually doing what needs to be done to motivate, during good times and during difficult times.

Let me try to give you some simple guidelines for exercising this leadership trait in your ministry. First you need to remember that motivation varies from person to person. What Ken Blanchard means when he says, "What motivates people is what motivates people," in reality means what motivates one person may not motivate another. This will probably be the greatest challenge you'll face when motivating your team.

First of all be aware of the possible reasons why people serve in a church or an organisation in order to determine their usefulness.

1. Their desire to pass on to others what they know

2. Their desire to be of help in a multitude of practical ways

3. The desire for a ministry in which they can exercise their talents and gifts

4. The desire for personal growth and development

5. The desire for recognition and a sense of achievement

6. The desire to learn how to do ministry

7. The desire for stimulation and something new

8. The desire to help people find Christ

9. The desire for Christian fellowship

How to keep them motivated

1. Show appreciation in little ways. A 'thank you' note, or half day off, a meal, a phone call to say thanks etc. can do wonders to keep your team motivated.

2. Create a stimulating environment where people are eager to

work and serve. Often the place of work can be very disheartening and pathetic.

3. Show recognition for work well done. Do this at special and well organised functions and make the rewards attractive.

4. Make sure that they are fulfilled in what they are doing and that they feel that the work they are doing is interesting and important. Do not assume too much.

5. Allow them to give you feedback about your own performance to determine if you are not contributing to some motivational problems.

6. Give them opportunity for achievements by helping them set achievable goals. People who produce good results feel good about themselves.

7. Give them responsibility for important tasks and even allow them to do what you like doing.

8. Help them measure how they are doing. Create an environment where feedback and evaluation is non-threatening and just part of growth and development.

9. Show concern for their personal needs, even if it means sacrificing time to do it. Feed them spiritually and be careful that you don't just use them. Feed their aspirations.

10. Allow for new challenges and opportunities in a changing environment.

11. Consider them as part of the team. Involve them in decision making, planning, implementing and evaluating ministry.

12. Take extra energy and time to minister to your individual team members. Find out how they are doing spiritually. If they are enjoying church life and if there are any personal struggles.

Demonstrate your genuine care for others by continually motivating them according to their unique needs in this regard.

Reflection

1. What motivates you?

2. Can you identify what motivates the people you lead?

3. How will you use that knowledge to build a strong team?

Part IX

LEADING THROUGH CHANGE

As servant leaders the answer to the question of **how** to lead is 'through service to God and others'. The answer to the question of **what** is leadership may be 'change'. Perhaps the essence of leadership is change. Maybe that's why Maxwell's often cited description of leadership touches a chord - 'Influence' may be the best way of combining elements of what and how when it comes to leadership (of course it leaves a lot of things unsaid and requires qualification etc. but as a kernel it might not be that bad). Transformational leadership remains the prevalent leadership model for our time. Have you noticed how many of the recent books and titles on leadership presume that the key outcome of leadership is transformation. It is almost as though this has become a self-evident truth regarding leadership and the focus has now switched to how to bring about holistic change: personal growth and development as a leader, change in the situation or context where leading occurs and change in the lives of those the leader leads.

81 Leading Your Organisation Through Change

Change is a fact of life for leaders and yet many are uncertain about whether change is a good thing or a necessary evil. Often change is forced upon us by external forces. These types of changes can be uncomfortable and complex. They demand the kind of leadership that can effectively respond to the rapid changes in the 21st Century. Funding problems, ineffective leadership, declining profits, drop in sales, increased competition, lack of resources, deregulation, consumer pressure, supplier problems, morale problems, absenteeism, high turnover of key people, internal politics, labour problems, mergers, takeovers, top management changes, spin-offs, reorganisation, divestiture, downsizing, new technology are daily occurrences and demand that we change.

Within an organization change can be threatening. Too often the view of top leadership demanding change varies considerably from that of front-line workers who may be unsure why change is even necessary. Senior leaders are concerned about the financial performance and usually require action quickly. Front-line employees do not have the day-to-day view of the business side of things. They want to do their job and want to know how the change will impact them personally. These two mindsets usually come into conflict and must be handled well.

Someone said, 'It is easier to start with a new crew than to transform the one you have'. For many, change is hard.

1. Some want others to change but they don't want to change themselves

2. Some are afraid of change and prefer to be passive

3. Some people have the will to change but not the skill to change

4. Some believe in the principle of change but find it hard to let go of the status quo

5. Some resist change for all kinds of emotional reasons

6. Some are prepared to change but are not actually ready for change

Manfred Kets de Vries describes what he refers to as the 5 C's of Change

1. **Concern** - people must experience a sense of concern about their present situation and daily frustrations.

2. **Confrontation** - people need to be confronted about the threat to their well-being and see new possibilities.

3. **Clarification** - people will be more willing to support when we clarify our intentions publicly. A process of dialogue may lead to further insights.

4. **Crystallisation** - people must clearly work through issues that have been envisioned.

5. **Change** - people are ready to change when they have a new mindset.

In 2001, after research with more than 700 companies undergoing change, Prosci concluded that the effective people dimension of change requires

1. **A**wareness of the need to change

2. **D**esire to participate and support the change

3. **K**nowledge of how to change

4. **A**bility to implement the change on a day-to-day basis

5. **R**einforcement to keep the change in place

The leadership challenges during change

1. Have a good reason for making the change/s

2. Involve people in the change

3. Create a shared commitment to change

4. Place a respected person in charge of the process

5. Provide training in new values and behaviour

6. Create transition management teams

7. Build attitudes, competencies and practices

8. Bring in outside help where necessary

9. Establish symbols of change

10. Improve and maintain performance

11. Acknowledge and reward people who contribute to the change

---

Reflection

Have you in the past had the challenge of leading an organisation through change? What were the results, and what would you do differently if you had to do it again?

---

82   The Leader as a Change Agent

It is difficult to work in situations where people constantly oppose any kind of change. I developed a relationship with the leadership team responsible for the managements of the city where I lived, and discovered they were 'tearing out their hair' as they sought ways to convince people about the need to change.

At times people want a new mayor, new pastor, and new Sunday School head and want them to be effective but they do not want the changes that go with it. Everyone will resist change that affects him or her. If you fold your arms one way, it's just plain uncomfortable and a nuisance to fold them the other way (try it). Why? Because we are creatures of habit. Change implies that people have to adjust their habits.

To be a leader is to be a change agent. To lead people in a church or organisation is asking them to change something. So a leader must be willing to face the problems of leading people through change. Because, according to Rick Warren, "all growth is change, all change is loss, and all loss is pain."

We reject change because of:

1. **Anxiety** - I'm afraid I cannot do this new thing.

2. **Loss** - Feel threatened. You worked hard to get where you are and losing financially, emotionally and reputationally is frightening.

3. **Anger** - My routine is threatened. My expertise is made irrelevant in the new.

4. **Doubt** - About the long-term success of the new way to do things.

5. **Jealousy** - Someone is better at this new thing than I am and younger.

6. **Fear** - Of the unknown.

7. **Introduction** - not sure of the intention of the person introducing change.

8. **Risks** - This is someone else's ideas or goals. Not so sure if it will work.

9. **Satisfaction** - A level of satisfaction with the existing way of doing things.

10. **Negative attitude** - Toward change in general

11. **Lack of respect** - people just have no faith in the leader. The leader failed them before.

   o   Followers need to know we live in an era of change, the rate of which is faster today than in the past.

   o   The leader must know what to change. Principles do not change but methods must be modernized.

   o   *All will face change. It is here to stay. It's unavoidable. The only thing we are assured of is 'change'.*

Change is Biblical. It is a common word in the Bible. In 2 Corinthians 3 the Apostle Paul talks about the work of the Holy Spirit in our lives. He said we would be changed from glory to glory, meaning we would be in the process of constant change. In Acts 9 and Acts 13 Paul introduces something radical. Those churches could also consist of Gentiles not only Jews. Jeremiah also saw that Jews could even prosper in Babylon, unheard of.

In Numbers 13:25.26 Joshua and Caleb believed that the Jews could even work effectively amid the Egyptians. Others only saw suffering and imprisonment.

To manage change you must have:

1.   The innovative urge

2.   An above-average passion for principle

3.   A need for affirmation that is much lower than average

4.   A high level of curiosity

5.   A track record of mastering failure

People accept change when:

1.   It appears to make sense and reasons are compelling.

2.   They are involved in the decision to change

3.   Their security needs are supported

4.   The implications are specific and clear

5.   Those affected approve the consequences

6.   The risks are minimised

Critical steps for overcoming the resistance to change

1. Give background information and describe why a change is necessary

2. Explain how the change will affect the member

3. Ask the member for questions about the change

4. Listen and respond openly to the member's question or comments

5. Ask the member for his or her help in making the change work

5 levels of change towards maturity

1. Knowledge - being exposed to new ideas, situations and emotions

2. Perspective - gaining perspective on the new. How does it fit in with that which I already believe

3. Conviction - being convinced that this is good, right, beneficial, needed and desired

4. Skills - gaining that which is needed to implement the new

5. Character - habitually existing in the new paradigm

Innovation and change

1. Identify, nurture and give opportunities for those who are creative to assist in the change

2. Be careful how you respond to new ideas. Do not react negatively but rather try to redirect

3. Challenge and thank God for those who help you create positive change

4. Avoid the copycat syndrome. We need more originals, not copy cats

5. Count the cost of change and budget for change carefully

6. Honour those who make a commitment to change

7. Be humble and not a know-it-all attitude. Be a willing leader

8. Give people permission to pay part of the price with you

9. Stay young in your thinking

Reflection

1. How will you go about managing your own resistance to change?

2. What stubborn resistance to change within you is robbing you of the benefits of change?

3. How will you apply your new knowledge to being an agent of change?

83   The Leader as a Vision Bearer

We sat in our staff meeting one day and somebody gave me a sheet of paper. It was sent to me by our newly appointed 16 year old dance leader, asking me if she could go ahead with her proposal on the sheet. What I saw on that piece of paper was a young leader with a very big vision.

> *"Vision is the ability to see what might be, rather than what is"*
> *- Geoff Rutter*

A vision statement for your church or organisation will describe the preferred or desired state. It is a description of how it will position itself in the future.

> *"Significant vision precedes significant success"*
> *- Fred Polak*

- Having vision forces us to take a stand for a preferred future.
- Having a vision helps leadership focus on the long-term perspective, and serve as a benchmark for evaluating actions.
- Having a vision gives momentum to the pioneering aspect of the ministry because it gives us something we are willing to take risks for.
- Having a vision helps create discontentment with the mediocrity of our current comfort zone.
- Having a vision keeps people motivated and on course.

> *Vision without action is merely a dream*
> *Action without vision just passes the time*
> *Vision with action can change the world - Joel Barker*

Every successful organization needs a vision

- That is clear
- That is divinely initiated
- That is tested
- That has limits
- That has been incubated

● That is written down

Vision and the leadership of Moses (Exodus 3:8)

1. It gave his people a true sense of destiny
2. It brought coherence to his people (Judges 21:25)
3. It bred endurance in them
4. It provided continuity for his people
5. It solved his identity problem (Ex 3:11)
6. It solved his authority problem (Ex 3:13)
7. It bridged the credibility gap (Ex 4:1)
8. It answered the ability problem (Ex 4:10)
9. It became the basis for his security (Numbers 12:1-16; 17:1)

"I pray that your inner vision may be flooded with light to enable you to see what hope the fact that he has called you gives you." (Ephesians 1:18 Barclay)

Reflection

1. What will you edit or add in your personal vision to more accurately align it with your inner vision?
2. In what ways will you have to improve your ability to be a vision giver?

84 Reviewing Your Traditions

In a 1978 Preachers Magazine, Ronald S. Combs tells a story about a young bride who was preparing her first meal for her husband. She had chosen to roast a large ham. Her husband walked into the kitchen just as she was cutting off a chunk from the end. Picking up the piece he asked, "Why did you cut this piece off?" With a befuddled look she replied, "Well I don't know, but my mother always did." Picking up the piece of ham, he led his wife into the living room to his mother-in-law and asked, "When you cook a ham, why do you cut this piece off." The mother, in turn, looked puzzled and replied, "Well, I don't know, but my mother always did." The curious man ushered the wife and mother-in-law with the piece of ham into the family car and proceeded to his wife's grandmother. He held up the piece of ham and asked her, "Why do you cut off this piece of ham? My wife says it's because her mom always did. And her mom says it's because you always did. Why?" With a twinkle in her eye, the wise old woman reached into a pantry, pulled out a well used cooking pan and answered, "Well honey, because it wouldn't fit in my pot."

Many traditions that rule our lives, churches or even businesses may in fact serve no practical purpose. The Bible warns us of traditions that we cling to which have nothing to do with the principles of God's Word. Jesus broke several traditions. He healed a man on the Sabbath and spoke to a woman publicly at a well. Many times it landed Him in trouble with the spiritual authorities. The Bible has something to say on the subject.

- **Ex. 12:1-3** Traditions were developed to remind people and highlight the religious significance of certain events.

- **Joshua 17:3-4** Moses put justice ahead of tradition and gave five women the land they deserved. Traditionally this was just for men.

- **Matt. 8:10-12** Jews so entrenched in religious traditions that they could not accept Christ and His new message.

- **Matt. 15:1-6** Jewish leaders elevated traditions to the same level as the Scriptures. Jesus rebukes them.

- **Rom. 4:10-12** Rituals and traditions do not earn blessings but serve as reminders of our faith.

Tradition is defined as the passing of beliefs, opinions, stories, statements or customs from one generation to the next by oral communication. It is any long-established method or practice.

I am not suggesting that we scrap all traditions - not at all. There are many fine traditions in societies, cultures and institutions, which are necessary and valuable. Certain traditions highlight the significance of certain holidays. Some people groups you identify by their traditions. Some traditions bring richness to a culture. In Madagascar, I admire many aspects of the funeral rituals and traditions. It creates a wonderful support system and makes it easier for some to part with a relative. There is also a quote by Combs, which illustrates my point: "If a tradition stands in the way of a positive change, then it is a yoke and not of any help."

This is rather a call to review our traditions. If they glorify God, promote freedom and growth, and enhance relationships, then build on them. If not, may be they have outlived their purpose.

Principles related to traditions:

1. Traditions should not violate the principles and commands of Scripture.

2. Traditions must help us to understand the Scriptures better and should not be turned into laws or doctrine.

3. Traditions should not stifle growth. For any kind of growth, change is needed and change could challenge some traditions. Therefore they must be looked at carefully and sensitively.

4. Traditions should not become an end in themselves. Some people love their traditional structures and liturgy more than they love God.

5. Traditions should serve as reminders for they are not important in themselves. They are outward symbols of something deeper or of an inner change.

6. Traditions should be evaluated against latest developments, trends and discoveries. Remember new programmes or activities in time become new traditions. When confronted keep the good and throw out the bad.

7. Traditions should not be criticised just because in your mind

they seem to be 'old fashioned'. It is possible to give new life to old traditional formats.

8. Take note, rigid guidelines may become established by traditions

9. Traditions should be reviewed by someone outside of our context. At times it is hard to recognise what it is doing because we have taken on its character. The Pharisees needed someone else, like Jesus.

Reflection

1. Identify some useless traditions in your life or organisation.

2. What will it take to challenge some of these traditions?

85 Developing a Positive Organizational Culture

The longer I'm involved in leadership within Youth For Christ the more I realize the influence 'culture' has within an organisation. Over the years I've seen leaders who could not fit because the organisation had a different personality and culture than they were accustomed to. I know of people who are uncomfortable with the informal, noisy and fun ways we do things at YFC. Sometimes a negative corporate culture can undermine or destroy a new leader's dreams. Some cultures stifle empowerment. Some produce effective but inefficient work. Some discourage initiatives by juniors. But there are other cultures where individuals grow and make great strides. In this Chapter we will attempt to explain briefly the concept of culture and to make suggestions for the development of a culture where people can flourish.

Culture defined

Some elements of a culture are values, beliefs, knowledge, traits, styles, expressions, symbols, customs, representations, language, space, rituals, routines, history, inner network, unconscious thoughts and assumptions. Culture is the way you behave and do things most of the time in your society, organisation or group.

"Corporate culture is the way insiders behave based on the values and group traditions they hold" (Hans Finzel).

Culture is important because it provides stability, it fosters certainty, it solidifies order and predictability and it creates meaning. (Weems)

Some general principles about culture

o   A healthy culture is needed to carry a great vision or strategy. Rules, policies and statements are not enough.

o   The symbols and images people see in a culture can give them confidence or can bring doubt in the things they do not see.

o · The elements of a culture are important to people and when these elements are changed they experience loss and react in the same way as they would to the death of a spouse.

Hans Finzel suggests the following principles for creating the right culture for Leaders to be effective

o   Never underestimate the power of corporate culture

o   Leadership must give attention to cultivating the culture

o   Only leadership can change culture

o   Many a fine person has perished in the wrong culture

How to create a strong culture where others can succeed

o   Create, articulate and sustain a compelling vision.

o   Understand and appreciate the uniqueness of your own culture

o   Keep your ears to the ground if you want to be a meaningful change agent

o   Allow your workers to flourish by giving them ownership, authority and a stake in the business/ministry

o   Model servant leadership and discard the traditional top down dictatorial leadership style.

o   Respect the members of your team as partners in the business/ministry

o   Articulate your values as often as you can

o   Be consistent with the vision and values you articulate

o   Learn how to give an appropriate response in the face of challenges

o   Get personally involved with the people you work with to ensure regular feedback

o   Show your commitment to needed change by your consistency and competence

---

Reflection

1. Identify and define the culture of your organisation.

2. What must change in your culture to help others succeed?

---

86 Preventing Institutional Dry-Rot

I have spent many years working with Youth for Christ International. Personally, I love this movement because it is capable of change. From time to time the leadership would unfold the work done to produce a new Strategic Ministry Focus . This process was made possible because its President brought together leaders who are prayer warriors, ready for a new paradigm, valuable innovators, 'off-the-wall' and original thinkers, copycat haters and gifted strategic thinkers who had the necessary energy to create and affect change.

The organization had a healthy discomfort with the status quo and wanted to:

● Keep its mission alive and 'life-changing'

● Live in the future and not the past

● Respond to the cries of today's young

● Be a dynamic, vibrant and growing organisation

● Be a united and caring family that can meet the demands of the 21st century

● Partner with others in the mammoth task of saving our young from the clutches and damnation of hell

Howard G. Hendricks in his book, 'Colour Outside the Lines', speaks about 6 symptoms that show deterioration in an institution.

1. Programmes are perpetuated that no longer meet the needs of people

2. More resources are spent on anniversaries than on the present and future

3. Maintenance and preservation takes precedent over growth and propagation

4. More concern is for reputation than responsibility (Jesus spent His energies with the people most of whom we try to avoid)

5. There is a greater concern for form than for function

6. There is a commitment to conformity rather than change

Many organisation, companies and churches that were once relevant, vibrant and dynamic are now shadows of their former selves.

John W. Gardner describes it so aptly, "Not because of stupidity or faulty beliefs, but because of internal decay and rigidification. They grow stiff in the joints. They get in a rut. They go to the seed."

Here are some fundamentals to help you prevent institutional dry rot.

1. Persistently communicate information that keeps unsettling people and moving towards change

2. Revisit and evaluate your original mission statements

3. Strategically plan for your organisation to be in business for a long time

4. Be committed to aggressive, innovative and creative methods to effectively meet the needs of the new generation

5. Spend a substantial amount of your resources on identifying, recruiting and the training of younger leaders within your movement, to meet the demands of the future.

"No eye has seen, no ear has heard, no mind has conceived what God has prepared for those who love him" (1 Cor. 2:9, NIV)

Reflection

1. In which ways are you and your organisation in a rut? How will you go about challenging the rot that has set in?

2. Rate you own ability to positively create the future, and to be a change agent for the good of all.

3. In your organisation, what would you change and what would you keep the same?

87   Innovation as a Leadership Challenge

On a recent visit to Cape Town I looked for a new computer gadget. I commented that it was way overpriced. The sales lady advised me to be patient and predicted a new design will be out in two months and the present price for the component I wanted could drop by 50%. We are living in a fast changing world and need to keep pace with developments and innovation, as it is the way of the future.

Some time ago my dad, who is a pastor, had a visiting missionary at his church. This guest told a story of a rural tribe in a remote village making handmade pouches for cell phones. We are truly becoming a global village and we need to embrace risk- taking, ongoing experimentation, the testing of boundaries and the challenge of assumptions.

A recent documentary on Madagascar, shown in South Africa, portrayed this vast island as still one of the poorest nations on earth. All around us we do see illiterate, starving families, growing poverty and marginalised groups. Yet, they have to deal with the growing emergence of cyber cafes, satellite links, the email and cell phones, in the bigger cities. It is not uncommon to see a modern car that is able to navigate for the driver and diagnose its automotive ills, lagging behind a cattle-driven cart.

We are living in a smarter, faster and technology-enabled world and need to find the most effective ways to bridge this gap and live out our mandate.

Innovation defined: Departing from the old and the use or introduction of new things, ideas and techniques

"If you continue doing what you are doing, you will get more of what you are getting." **Howard G. Hendricks**

Rodney Thorne, a friend of mine, commented "If you always do what you always did you always get what you always got".

Our challenge therefore, as leaders, is
1. To create an environment of innovation
2. To create resources to enable innovation

3. To invest in people to maintain innovation

4. To disciple, mentor and oversee the priceless supply of talent around you

5. To become future-orientated, anticipating questions that will be asked in 5 years' time

6. To network, which is a leading tool in developing a culture of development

7. To frequently change location or surroundings as it produces the highest form of innovation

8. To reward new, good and workable ideas

9. To allow for failure and mistakes in order to go right back and do it better

10. To demonstrate innovation in practice

11. To minimise rules and regulations that stifle innovation

12. To establish partnership in innovation

13. To support and nurture innovative initiatives

14. To showcase innovative projects

15. To create an environment where people can dream and turn those dreams into reality

'There is great potential in dreams, and the cost is free' - Byrd Baggett

Reflection

1. Identify some of the ways in which you can keep your leadership fresh and cutting edge.

2. In which ways are you holding onto the past and preventing moving into the future?

88 Staying in touch with your people

Louis Gerstner attributed the historic turnaround of IBM to the rediscovery of 'customer-focus' that became a key element of IBM'S mission.

In our ministry (YFC) one of our core values has been to hear what our members have to say about the movement and how they would like to see the YFC handed to them in the forthcoming years. We recognise the importance of having a 'connectedness' with our younger generation of leaders.

The more I study the parables of Jesus and the customs of the time, the more I am amazed at how relevant his revelations were. No wonder they flocked to hear him, for:

o He spoke their language

o He listened to them

o He understood their struggles

o He answered their questions

o He walked where they walked

o He ate with them

o He showed a genuine interest in them

o He made them feel safe enough to be transparent

o He gave them hope

Tom Marshall in his book, 'Understanding Leadership', says it so aptly."…Leaders not only have to be out in front of the people, they also have to stay in touch with the people. If leaders get too far out in front, the people will lose touch with them, and even more important, they will lose touch with the people. Leaders in other words have to be reaching out to worthwhile objectives but they have always to hold those goals in one hand and their people in the other so that they can judge or evaluate the likely compatibility or resonance between them."

By being in touch

1. You will have a better understanding of people's struggles and needs

2. You will have insight to the kind of leadership style they need.

3. You will have opinions and ideas to work with

4. You will have an opportunity to bounce off your opinions and ideas

5. You will have a good sense in how to guide and equip your people

6. You will have the know-how to match their abilities and strengths

7. You will have first-hand knowledge of people's perceptions and aspirations

8. You will have a better chance of putting compatible teams together

9. You will have wisdom in how to serve better

10. You will have a greater sensitivity and care about those you lead.

Some practical tips

1. Make time to socialise with people without discrimination

2. Master the art of listening - you're not the expert on everything.

3. Have a tolerance for diverging views

4. Interact with significant persons - explore their thinking and dreams.

4. Take an interest in what interests others

6. Realise that everyone, to the lowest rank has something to contribute

7. Keep in touch with people who generate original thought

8. Don't be threatened by feedback.

9. Invite others to help you solve problems.

10. Allow younger staff to tutor you - your know-how could be obsolete.

Reflection

1. What practical steps have you taken to ensure that you stay in touch with your people?

2. If you have difficulty in this area, what must change for you to be real and transparent enough to interact closely with your people?

89 Servicing Your Clients

We all have clientele that we serve. To a pastor it is his members, leaders, deacons, and church council. To a businessperson it is the one who buys his product, personnel, suppliers, partners, shareholders and Board of directors. In my job at Youth for Christ, it is the young people we serve, staff, volunteer workers, Board members, supporters, my colleagues and those who have oversight.

Your clients are all those who have an effect on your organisation.

Some time back I read 'Who says Elephants can't Dance' by **Louis V. Gerstner**, Jr. It was about the historic turnaround of IBM. I jotted down all his comments about client service as I felt it was the main thread of his book.

o   Convince clients you are serving their interest

o   Place yourself in the shoes of your clients

o   Listen to them and deliver what they expect

o   Show them that you care

o   Find out what they think about you

o   Become aggressive in the client/server arena

o   Make things happen to serve your clients

o   Bring solutions to clients

o   Become attentive to your clients

o   Serve them and not control them

o   Develop products that serve the client's needs

o   Measure the satisfaction level of your clients

o   Organise your resources around customers

o   Deliver working solutions to clients

o   Make your business service and not just the product

o   Move decision-making closer to your clients by decentralising

o   Conduct comprehensive client surveys

o   Focus the talents and efforts of your group outside your company and not on one another. Start winning in the marketplace.

In South Africa, management consultants such as John Rae, Theo Jansen and others have developed a course on 'Preparing for, Implementing and Managing a Superior Client Care Culture in your company'. The following points are a summarized form of their manual in point form.

o   Superior service is the competitive edge

o   Superior service is an attitude

o   Superior service means an obsession with quality and reliability

o   Superior service means identifying your clients

o   Superior service creates a reputation and generates good stories

o   Superior service has a concern for 'first impressions'

o   Superior service means continuous improvements and developments

o   Superior service means listening to your clients

o   Superior service means empowering your staff to serve the clients

o   Superior service means measuring periodically how you are doing

o   Superior service means holding everyone accountable

o   Superior service means catching your people doing something right

o   Superior service is a management issue and this is a priority

Client service is all about reliability, responsiveness, competence, access, courtesy, communication, credibility, reputation, understanding, quality, care and presentation.

"Superior client service creates positive stories, and positive stories pay off." 'Preparing for, Implementing and Managing a Superior Client Care Culture in your company'

Do yourself a favour and read the stories of Jesus. Talk about superior service! No wonder He said, "Your attitude must be like my own, for I the Messiah, did not come to be served, but to serve and to give my life as a ransom for many".

Reflection

1. Who are your direct clients, what is their understanding of service, and what service levels do they require?

2. What measurement systems do you have in place to accurately assess your service effectiveness, and what areas of improvement and excellence do these highlight?

Part X

OVERCOMING ADVERSITY

There is a certain vulnerability that comes with leadership. There are dangers, perils and conflicts commonly associated with the role. There are also, on occasion, more sinister challenges that arise from opposition and people who might even be considered 'enemies'. It takes the development of a strong character and the ability to persevere in order to be able cope with these. It also requires a strong inner strength that comes out of principled personal decision making. A leader must learn to deal well with adversity in order to accomplish their God-given purposes and dreams.

90   Overcoming Discouragement in the Ministry

How does a leader deal with discouragement? Perhaps it is because they see little growth in their ministry. There seems to be little reward for their efforts. People don't want to change and they are tired of trying. Things are not going their way. They desperately need help but everyone is too busy. Problems are hitting them from all sides. They just feel that no one appreciates their sacrifice. Sometimes they feel guilty for saying no and they end up doing things that they just hate doing. What they hate most are the reports of colleagues that make them feel like a failure. Their family is struggling to make ends meet. It's difficult to forgive themselves for past failure. To top it all, they have no one really that they feel they can talk to. I suppose the list goes on and on. In my son's 'Youth' Bible I read how you can spot a discouraged person: "He or she looks like an old, worn-out, broken-down car on the side of the road, bonnet raised weakly in surrender". How does a leader fight this loss of motivation and find the energy to go on?

I have come up with five headings to cover all I have read and experienced over the years on the subject.

1. Take care of your own mental and spiritual health

Plan to have 'time out'. If you have no time to read, to relax, to have fun, to be with the family or go for a short holiday then something is wrong. You need physical, intellectual and spiritual stimulation or you will pay a price and become stagnant in ministry. Some people feel guilty for taking breaks or reading a book. No one else is going to take responsibility for your growth and development. It's up to you.

2. Cultivate friendships

When last did you spend time with a friend? Are you expecting all your social needs to be met by the people you minister to? Find individuals who can stimulate you. Allow yourself the time to be with people outside your sphere of ministry. In YFC I have discovered that if you do not periodically break away from the young people you serve, then you take on their emotional hang-ups and become just like them. Cultivate friendships, for it can get lonely in ministry.

3. Find the root cause of your discouragement

What is sapping your emotional energy? Is it the long hours, your environment, the cultural adaptations, the sudden low after a high, lack of job satisfaction, lost opportunities, your inability to keep commitments, unrealistic expectations, the unwarranted criticism, unfulfilled dreams, lack of skills for the job, the slow growth, ongoing conflict, or your insecurities?

4. Never to give up

God has designed our experiences for specific reasons. Fulfilment, development or growth comes with a price. We want the right outcomes but not at a cost. In my discouragement God could be teaching me real ministry and service. People tend to lose their purpose during times of discouragement. The apostle Paul had every reason to give up but knew how to overcome discouragement (2 Corinthians 4:7-18).

5. Keep your focus

Do yourself a favour and read the account of Nehemiah. He had enough to discourage him for a lifetime - ridicule, violent plots, and physical exhaustion but he knew where to focus - on the power and ability of God (Nehemiah 4:1-21; Nehemiah 6:15-16). Concentrate on God and not on the obstacles you face. Do what you can do by drawing from His strength. Stop offloading on to people about your lot in life. Get rid of your eagerness for everyone to feel sorry for you rather open up to God and tell Him. God will give you the resources and strength to carry on. Do not lose faith and neglect your life of prayer or you will lose God's role for you.

Reflection

1. Be honest. What is causing the most discouragement in leading others right now, and how are you going to deal with it?

2. How will you recognise when others have lost their motivation, and how will you deal with those situations?

91 The Loneliness of Leadership

It's lonely at the top! Many leaders have experienced this reality. This is not to suggest that leaders are so much higher than anyone else that they have become distant. That's positional or hierarchical leadership thinking and not a serving leader mentality. Rather, the sense of loneliness comes from the unique roles and responsibilities of leadership. Carrying the vision includes being in the frame of mind that is ahead of where everyone else is. Taking initiative sometimes means sticking your neck out. Leading the way means being in front. Many of the worlds great leaders were known for taking extended time to be alone and reflect on their leadership.

Geoff Rutter, in his article 'The Loneliness of Command' (Edge Magazine 2001), considers the issue of loneliness in leadership by looking at the life of Jesus. He starts by quoting Machiavelli, who said, "There is no more delicate matter to take in hand, nor more dangerous to conduct, nor more doubtful of success, than to step up as a leader in the introduction of changes. For he who innovates will have for his enemies all those who are well off under the existing order of things, and only lukewarm supporters in those who might be better off under the new".

Being a leader implies 'being in front' - and often this means being on your own. In our rapidly changing world, leaders have to preside over change, and perhaps sacrifice popularity in doing so - and this requires the rare quality of courage.

Jesus is a good example of someone who knew the cost of leadership.

- In John 10:4, He identifies with the normal Palestinian shepherd's style when He said, "the shepherd goes ahead of the sheep", as opposed to driving them from behind.

- When He faced the cross, His back was to Galilee, relative security, a childhood home, happy memories - ahead was conflict and death. He longed for human support and encouragement, but no one could identify with His purpose.

- In Matthew 26:40 we hear His anguished cry for human help in the garden of Gethsemane: "Could you men not watch with me for one hour?"

- On the Cross, He was on His own, even forsaken by His Father.

- In Matthew 26:56, Jesus lost His popularity to the extent that, when the crunch came, "all the disciples deserted Him and fled."

- Sometimes Jesus withdrew because He was so absorbed in His Father's purpose. He often sent the crowds away because of His need for solitude.

A Bishop by the name of Fulton Sheen remarked, "When you are getting kicked from the rear it means you're in front". There is no doubt that one of the penalties of leadership is 'positional solitude'. Leaders often have to take unpopular positions, and will invariably alienate some people, as they attempt to lead change.

Reflection

1. Think of an occasion when you felt very lonely in your leadership.

2. What advice would you give to others about this?

92 Handling Criticism

Some of us in leadership positions find it hard to handle criticism. By criticism I don't mean helpful and constructive feedback, but rather mean-spirited destructive behaviour. Criticism may come from enemies, competitors, colleagues, superiors, our team, the community, and even our family. It affects people in different ways. Today there are those who suffer physically and emotionally because of things that were said about them. Others have just cracked down under the strain. Then there are those who dread facing meetings for fear of criticism. Many have just resigned because they cannot deal with it. All leaders are at risk of being pronounced guilty without having a chance to explain or defend themselves. Gossip, rumours, innuendos, exaggerations and speculations are just part of the package when you enter the arena of leadership. According to Arlo Walker, "Coping with critics, complainers, and even the not-so-occasional loud mouth is routine in ministry…" As a leader we must either get tough or we will be destroyed.

We often respond negatively to our critics

1. We are quick to confront and do it out of anger

2. We return the criticism

3. We withdraw immediately

4. We take it personally and give up

5. We justify our actions

6. We get angry, hurt or bitter and feel betrayed

7. We go around lobbying to get others on our side

8. We ask our critics, sarcastically, to do better

Why do leaders get criticised?

1. Leaders are visionaries and change agents and people generally do not handle change well. They prefer the status quo

2. Leaders will experience this when the good days are over and things are going badly and times are getting tough

3. Leaders usually attempt new challenges while existing goals are only partially accomplished

4. Leaders will experience this when people do not know what is going on

5. Leaders at times have different perceptions than others

6. Leaders abuse their power and people are manipulated and hurt

7. Leaders face people who are just critical by nature

8. Leaders face those who are just jealous

The Apostle Paul's critics

Paul had a fair amount of criticism and suffered much at the hands of the opponents of the gospel. Kenneth Prior in his book 'Perils of Leadership' has a great chapter on Paul and his critics. He shows how they tried to undermine his ministry in every way. Often he had to defend his motives, methods, message, character, appearance and his authority as an apostle. In 2 Cor. 1:15-17, he defends his integrity against those who moaned that he did not visit them and in 2 Cor. 12:14-18 he defends himself against questions raised about his handling of money. In 2 Cor. 10:10, he had to deal with accusations of being inconsistent.

The way Paul dealt with criticism

1. He had a high view of his office but kept a low view of himself Eph 3:8; 1 Cor. 15:9-10

2. He knew where his authority came from 1 Cor. 4:1

3. He submitted and remained under the authority and judgement of God and not those he ministered to 1 Cor. 4:3-5

4. He admitted his faults and weaknesses 2 Cor. 10:3; 2 Cor. 4:7

How to handle criticism

1. Do not reject it out of hand

2. Be grateful for it keeps us humble

3. Do not let it sap your energy and strength or demoralise you

4. Do not let it control you or rule your life

5. Do not personalise it

6. Find the reason for the criticism

7. Do not give as good as you get

8. Do not respond when you are angry and emotional

Reflection

1. What forms of criticism do you experience and how do you currently handle that criticism?

2. In the light of what you now know, which areas of handling criticism would require improvement to allow you to handle it with maturity?

---

93 Dealing with Envy and Jealousy

As a leader we want nothing more than for the ministry and organization we lead to successful, to benefit and to have its needs met. Sometimes it is hard to see others around us prosper while we continue to struggle. Some months back I really had to check my heart because I could not understand why God provided for a particular need in another leader's ministry. I had that same need and had prayed for years but felt that God wasn't coming through for me. I thought God was unfair.

Questions to consider

o   How do we really deal with other people's or organisation's success?

o   Do we have the right to tell God whom to bless and not to bless?

o   Do we recognise that we have at times this spirit of envy or jealousy?

o   Do we recognise the effects it has on relationships and the workplace?

Jealousy as seen in the Scriptures:

1. Murderous Jealousy

Gen 4:3-8 - Cain jealous of his brother, Abel whose offering was accepted by God. He eventually killed Abel.

2. Jealous of a young promising leader

1Sam. 19:1-23 - King Saul desperately attempts to destroy David because of jealousy. He cannot stand the adoration of the women and crowds of this young valiant warrior.

3. Jealous for power

Isaiah 14: 13-14 - Lucifer is vying for position and wanted to be like the 'most high'. This led to his destruction and exit from heaven.

4. Religious jealousy

Acts 13:44 - Almost the whole city heard the Word of God - the Jews filled with jealousy and spoke against Paul. Paul was stoned and left for dead.

5. Jealous in spite of privileged position

Luke 15:28 - 31 - In the story of the prodigal son, the elder son became very jealous because his father gave a homecoming celebration. As the older son and heir, his jealousy made him forget what he had.

Are we any different?

Some times we covet other people's good looks, academic success, personality, material possessions, positions, promotions, privileges, which leads to a spirit of envy and jealousy. We then make unkind remarks and destructive comments and wallow in self pity, anger, bitterness and even depression.

Some cautions

- o Recognise that envy/jealousy are strong, vicious emotions
- o Recognise that you are being crippled by an immature and self-centred emotion
- o Recognise that it could retard the growth and development of others
- o Recognise when you have that spirit and deal with it

Proverbs 27:4 "Jealousy is more dangerous and cruel than anger"

Proverbs 14:30 "A sound heart is life to the body, but envy is rottenness to the bones"

"We're blasted by anger and swamped by rage, but who can survive jealousy?" *The message.*

What to do:

1. Be content. Phil 4:12-13 - "I have learned the secret of being content in any and every situation, whether well fed or hungry, whether living in plenty or in want. I can do everything through Him who gives me strength."

2. Let us die to this unrighteous fruit of darkness - Phil 2:3-4. Seek deliverance from envy and jealousy.

3. Encourage, serve, affirm and set others free to become what God intends them to be.

4. Look for the good in others, pray for them, and appreciate the good qualities in others and how God is coming through for them.

Someone said:

When you hear your brother is made Bishop - smile and bless him.

Reflection

1. Be honest with yourself about situations in which you have been jealous and envious. How did you deal with those and what would you change, if you had to do them over again?

2. What causes you to be jealous, and how will you prevent jealousy from taking hold of your heart?

94   When You Think of Quitting

I was taken by surprise one day when I got a call from an associate, "Sorry David, but I quit, I'm sorry hey! Thanks for everything." The call took me by surprise, messed up my schedule but it got me thinking.

Maybe today you are considering putting in your resignation because of constant setbacks in your relationships and aspirations. You want out because you are hurt, discouraged or disappointed and you just have no more energy left to try.

At times there are legitimate reasons for leaving or God is leading you on to something new, but often you need to carefully consider the following, before doing so. Make sure that you think through these truths before quitting:

1. Recognise that there is no perfect place

    When I was little I heard my dad say from the pulpit, "If you're looking for the perfect church, don't join it or you'll spoil it". Most problems are common to every church or ministry because basically they are all made up of 'sinners in the process of becoming'. What you see is never really what you get. I know of folk who left their church because they were unhappy with the worship. They found a mega church with great music but ended up leaving the country because of major problems they encountered with the pastor's wife in their new church.

2. Recognise your need to learn and grow

    We all know that failure and success make up experience and that is the only way we grow. In ministry, things don't always go your way. Paul charges Timothy in 2 Tim. 3 about his life of endurance, persecution and sufferings and all the things he had to go through to attain a life of godliness. Most times when you quit you stunt your own growth. Consider Hebrews 10:35-38 and Luke 9:62 before doing so. Sometimes you need to change instead of the situation changing for you.

3. Recognise the positive things happening around you

    The terrorist attack on America has given the world some real insight to that country. We have been exposed to another side of the USA. Their commitment, sacrifice, determination, loyalty and camaraderie. All of a sudden their eyes were off Hollywood and Michael Jordan and their real heroes became the firemen and policemen. Sometimes our few problems are expanded in our minds and make us oblivious of the wonderful things that are happening around us.

4. Recognise there are alternatives to quitting

Before making a decision, talk to someone and seek help and healing. Take a short break and get some perspective. Examine your workload and delegate. Deal Biblically with relationship issues. Make changes to your lifestyle. Bring balance back into your life.

5. Recognise there are those who do care

Daily when I read my emails and letters, I am constantly amazed at the amount of love and care in the Christian community. Sometimes the busyness, pressure or financial concerns of others makes them unaware of the crisis in your life and it seems as if they don't care. Years in ministry and the lessons of others have taught me otherwise. When you quit you begin to realise how much people care and how much they love you.

Reflection

1. What are some of the reactions you have seen from leaders when one of their people quit?

2. Are you aware of somebody who wants to quit, and you know they have not received proper counsel? What will you do to assist?

---

95 Leaders Need Friends During Tough Times

When I was recovering from surgery done on my arm, my family was thousands of miles away. I longed for them to be around but instead God gave me wonderful friends who really went the extra mile. They gave me much more than I could have ever expected. None of us can survive without friends. I find it ironic that leaders who deal with people all the time are often 'lone rangers'. Leaders cannot make it on their own.

David and Jonathan portray a wonderful picture of friendship **(1Sam 18:1-4; 23:16-18; 2 Sam 1:17-27; 9:1-13)**

1. Their friendship is cemented by a covenant commitment to each other.

2. David needed Jonathan who gave him invaluable support and 'strengthened his hand in God' during some of his darkest days.

3. Jonathan showed spiritual maturity by accepting that God had chosen David and not him (the king's son) to rule Israel—it was a very secure relationship.

4. Jonathan, at great risk to himself, tried to reconcile David with King Saul by speaking well of him.

5. Jonathan remained true and loyal to David as he persevered through very difficult periods in his life.

We all need friends...

o   To tell us the hard truth

o   Who will sacrifice for us

o   To help us be successful in our endeavours

o   To be there when we are discouraged

o   To help us persevere through the tough times

o   To steer us out of trouble

o   Whom we can rely on

o   To become our confidants

o   Who will add value to our lives

o   Who are genuinely concerned about us

o   Who believe in our ministry

o   Who will allow us to vent our feelings

o   Who won't allow success to go to our heads

o   To pray with

These are some things I'm learning from many years in leadership.

1.   Build friendships with a group of peers at a similar level of leadership to help you avoid taking on some of the immature characteristics of those you minister to, especially if they are young people.

2.   Be accountable and committed to a group where you can foster good friendships, socialise and have fun.

3.   Develop interests outside of ministry or work.

4.   Have a prayer partner.

5.   Make your spouse your most intimate friend.

Pictures of those who needed friends during their most trying days

1.   Job's three friends who decide to be by his side during his most severe trials. Job 2:11

2.   Ruth after losing her husband commits herself to her mother-in-law, Naomi. A picture of love, faithfulness and friendship. Ruth 1:14-18

3.   Jesus who needed His three closest disciples by His side, during His time of agony in the Garden of Gethsemane. Matt 26:36-38

4.   Mary and Martha who needed their friend, Jesus when they lost their brother, Lazarus. John 11:1-16

5.   Paul had two friends who risked their lives for him. Romans 16:3,4

Reflection

1.   Describe your circle of friends. Do they display the maturity of leadership required to challenge you to grow?

2.   How regularly and deliberately do you indulge in "hanging out" with peers?

96   Achieving Success in Work and Love

Many people believe that you cannot be both successful in your career and family life. To be fully committed to one, the other must suffer. They say you must make a choice between the two. Well, McGinnis in his book 'The Balanced Life' takes a different position, believing that you can be a success both at work and at home. He maintains that "people with the best family lives and the best friend-ships…make the best mark in their careers." He also quotes Tolstoy, "One can live magnificently if one knows how to work and how to love, to work for the person one loves, and to love one's work." The book explores four laws of success in work and love. I would like to take the liberty of summarising his ideas to help those of us who are trying to integrate a whole range of work priorities with relationships and a healthy home life.

1. **The first law is Commitment** - A survey showed that those who were successful in both career and relationships had one thing in common - a passionate intensity called commitment. They know how to stay in the race and yet know how to keep relationships alive. Spending long hours at work is justified if we give the same commitment to the people we love. Commitment will mean learning to do a few things well instead of spreading ourselves too thin. We will focus on our gifts instead of trying to be the guru in everything. We will build on our strengths and learn to enjoy what we do (Ecc. 9:10). What we do will also reflect our scale of values. We won't be easily sidetracked. Commitment is seen in our goals, associations, time spent with our family, creation of our destiny, in problem solving, in finding a course between boredom and stress, in going the second mile and in replenishing our spiritual reserves.

2. **The second law is Discipline** - Discipline will help us to suc-ceed in work and love. It helps you not to quit during tough times. Some bury themselves in their work when they have problems in relationships and vice versa. Disciplined people are not guided by feelings. They deal with issues. They set positive attainable goals and build in rewards. They keep accurate records of their progress and build up a tolerance for pain. They fight procrastination tendencies. Disciplined people keep com-mitments.

3. **The third law is Collaboration** - "There is no such thing as a self-made person. You will reach your goals only with the help of others" (George Shinn). We grow and we accomplish the most in the company of loved ones, co-workers, colleagues and trusted advisors. We won't survive if we try to go too far alone. "We human beings can survive the most difficult circumstances if we are not forced to stand alone" (James Dobson). Learn to ask for help and to believe in people. Believe in the mentoring system and share power with others. Let us help our subordinates grow and share the credit and rewards with others. Understand the value of communication, having fun together, the need to belong, celebrating success together, dealing with conflicts and taking responsibility for quality.

4. **The fourth law is Adaptability** - Those who have a dislike for innovation and who resist change will find success in the 21st century bleak. You will also find it impossible to keep the balance. Things are shifting so fast we need to be quick to seize opportunities in both relationships and our careers. Keep growing and welcome change. "Long term relationships require constant attention and adaptability" (Samuel Johnson). Learn to improvise work and love, becoming more supportive and meet each other's needs. Take advantage of change. Do not let tight schedules cause you to miss out on the best moments of life. Learn to keep things stable in relationships while going through change in some career move. Learn the art of 'comeback'. Recognise the difference between failing and calling yourself a failure. Face your mistakes, persevere and be a perpetual learner.

Reflection

1. Evaluate how well you are doing in the four areas above on a scale of 1 to 10.

2. Which of these laws of success challenge you the most, and what are you going to do to live a balanced life?

97 Learning to have Times of Fun and Refreshment

My secretary returned from her month's vacation and greeted me with a message from her doctor that said 'She is suffering from extreme fatigue'. Seating herself at her desk, she opened her bag and out came the missing calculator and files we thought we mislaid the past month. She had chosen to continue some of her work responsibilities while on leave and did not take a break. Now, unfortunately, she was physically facing the consequences.

Charles Swindoll has a great chapter in his book 'Strengthening your Grip' on the subject of leisure. This is what he says: "Many have cultivated such an unrealistic standard of high-level achievement that a neurotic compulsion to perform, to compete, to produce, to accomplish the maximum has taken control of their lives."

Myron Rush, who wrote 'Managing to be the Best', says "Learn to play as hard as you work…all work and no play will lead to disaster someday."

It is a shame that

- Some leaders boast of not having taken a vacation for years
- Some leaders can't relax or enjoy a weekend away without calling the office
- Some leaders feel that they cannot afford to go on vacation
- Some leaders think they are indispensable
- Some leaders feel guilty for taking time out to relax
- Some leaders work till they are burnt out and wonder why they are still exhausted after a month's forced break.

There are few work ethic myths we must dispel:

- That burnout is proof of our deep level of commitment - not true!
- That fatigue is next to godliness - not true!
- That the more tired we are the more we earn God's approval - not true!

Many of us have learnt how to work and in the process have forgotten how to have fun

- We need to make every effort to develop interests and activities away from work
- Play, fun, rest and leisure need a proper place of dignity and to become part of our lifestyle
- We need to learn to enjoy the things we do - even our work

Having fun

- Keeps us in balance.
- Is vital for positive relationships
- Reminds us we are human and more alike than different
- Brings refreshment and relaxation
- Helps in times of stress and brings a certain amount of release
- Releases the creative juices and at times stimulates the mind

Some other observers of fun and refreshment

1. Alan Loy McGinnis says in 'The Balanced Life', "Groups with good morale recognise that a certain amount of relaxation and frivolity is even more crucial when the group is under stress and working long hours."

2. Patty Marler and Jan Bailey Mattia in 'Time Management Made Easy', comment about enjoying the things we do: "Plan to treat yourself when you finish a project you didn't like, hum to yourself while waiting in line to pay your bills, or tickle your baby as you change her dirty nappy. No task has to be unbearable, and it is your choice to make it fun. If you make unpleasant tasks fun, imagine how great interesting tasks will be!"

3. Geoffrey Moss in 'Survival Skills for New Managers' states, "Do more of the things you enjoy. Try to spend more time with your family. Don't take yourself too seriously. Budget your time so you have more time for social activities and fun."

4. In 'Getting things done' by Alan C. Bliss he states, "Leisure is fun only when you can relax without feeling guilty, knowing that you've earned a good rest".

5. Charles R. Swindoll's comments on Proverbs 17:22, "I'd rather my brood remember me as the dad who tossed their mother fully clothed into the swimming pool (and lived to tell the story!), than the preacher who frowned too much, yelled too loud, talked too long.... and died too young."

6. Gordon MacDonald says in 'Restoring your spiritual passion' that the literal meaning of Exodus 31:17 is "And God rested and refreshed himself".

7. Jesus demonstrates this principle. He deliberately gets away from the crowds to rest. He enjoys special times out with His disciples. He is seen at a wedding, in the market place, on the shores, resting in a boat and socializing in the community (and getting criticised for it). Not once is it recorded that Jesus worked to a frenzy and needed counseling for emotional burn out.

Reflection

1. What do you do to have fun, and do you believe in any myths regarding hard work and fun?

2. What will you have to do or change in order to maintain balance?

---

98   Dealing with Stress

I am learning that being in the ministry is no guarantee that we are excluded from the effects of stress. In the ministry most of us are in people-helper roles and are more prone to physical and emotional depletion. No doubt it also leads to spiritual exhaustion. There is such a thing as good stress, such as a joyous occasion but bad stress leads to distress and in extreme cases to burnout. As leaders we need to understand the causes of stress before we can give counsel to our followers.

Causes of stress include:

- Hectic workload, schedule or lifestyle
- Being under-utilised
- Insufficient skills for the job and role clarity
- Change
- Lack of outlet or relaxing hobby
- Too much emotional involvement and relationship problems
- Management or leadership problems
- Inability to take breaks
- Unhealthy diet, inadequate sleep, chronic illness or disease
- Physical environment
- Feelings of insecurity or unfounded fears

Common symptoms of stress are:

- Deadlines are not being met
- The quality of work deteriorates
- The commitment and creativity reduces
- Frequent absenteeism, lateness or spells of sick leave
- Increased levels of complaints from members or clients
- Apathy concerning anything new
- Deteriorating inter-personal relations

Help your team manage their stress by:

1. Assisting them to manage themselves, their jobs and future

2. Giving guidance on health, diet, sleep or relaxation and leisure

3. Improving the work environment

4. Promoting teamwork and inter-personal skills development

5. Putting teams together that are compatible

6. Ensuring reasonable deadlines

7. Redesigning jobs

8. Clarifying roles and objectives

9. Encouraging balanced life-styles

I received a list of 37 Stress Reducers from a friend who runs a development agency called 'Winning Edge Developments'. Here they are:

1. Pray

2. Go to bed on time

3. Get up on time so you can start the day unrushed

4. Say no to projects that won't fit into your time schedule or that will compromise your mental health

5. Delegate tasks to capable others

6. Simplify and unclutter your life

7. Allow extra time to do things and to get to places

8. Pace yourself. Spread out big changes and difficult projects over time; don't lump the hard things all together

9. Take one day at a time

10. Separate worries from concerns. If a situation is a concern, find out what God would have you to do and let go of the anxiety

11. If you can't do anything about a situation, forget it

12. Live within your budget; don't use credit cards for ordinary purchases

13. Have back-ups; an extra car key in your wallet, an extra house key buried in the garden, extra stamps, etc.

14. K.M.S (Keep mouth shut). This single piece of advice can prevent an enormous amount of trouble

15. Do something for the Kid in you everyday

16. Carry a Bible with you to read while waiting in line

17. Get enough exercise

18. Eat right

19. Get organised so everything has its place

20. Listen to a tape while driving that can help improve your quality of life

21. Write thoughts and inspirations down

22. Everyday, find time to be alone

23. Having problems? Talk to God on the spot. Try to nip small problems in the bud

24. Don't wait until it is time to go to bed to try and pray

25. Make friends with godly people

26. Keep a folder of favourite Scriptures on hand

27. Remember that the shortest bridge between despair and hope is often a good, "Thank you, Heavenly Father!"

28. Laugh

29. Laugh some more!

30. Take your work seriously, but yourself, not at all.

31. Develop a forgiving attitude (most people are doing the best they can)

32. Be kind to unkind people (they probably need it the most)

33. Sit on your ego

34. Talk less, listen more

35. Slow down

36. Remind yourself that you are not the general manager of the universe

37. Every night before bed, think of one thing you're grateful for that you've never been grateful for before.

Reflection

1. Are you aware of the sources of stress in your life? What causes the most stress in your life?

2. Name some ways in which stress negatively impacts on your effectiveness as a leader.

3. What will you do to reduce your stress?

99 Casting Burdens in the Right Direction

I often hear about discouraged leaders who cannot handle the enormous strain and difficulties in the workplace. In 1 Peter 5:1-7, Peter is addressing the leadership in Asia Minor. The whole context of this passage hinges on leadership. Verse 2 *"Be shepherds of God's flock"*, viz. elders/supervisors.

Peter reminds the elders about their role which is that of a shepherd. Shepherds tend sheep. I think Peter used the analogy of a shepherd because he remembered being confronted by Jesus after his denial. Jesus said if you love me then feed my lambs. The primary task of a shepherd is to look out for the welfare of those committed to their leadership.

There are certain temptations that leaders face:

1. **The feeling that you are doing others a big favour.** Not being willing to lead

2. **Serving with wrong motives.** For the perks that come with the position

3. **Ending up being a complainer**. Because people are not responding to our leadership the way we expect them to respond

4. **Feeling superior to others.** 'Lording' over others and allowing gaps between us and those we lead

Christ should be our example of shepherding - in verse 1 Peter says that he was a witness of the way Christ led His people. It was a road of suffering - it was demanding, tedious and there was a price to pay. We should not forget why we are leading. We are witnesses and partakers of the glory of Christ. It comes with the job.

Heb 2:10 "In bringing many sons to glory it was fitting that God, for whom and through whom everything exists, should make the author of their salvation perfect through suffering."

Now in this context Peter says to leaders: "Casting all your cares upon Him, for He cares for you" (verse 7). Peter understood casting as a fisherman. At one time Jesus told Peter and fellow fishermen to cast their nets on the other side, i.e. to cast in the right direction.

Peter, as an elder in the Jerusalem church made this link between shepherding and casting. As leaders/shepherds of God's flock we must cast our anxieties and struggles in the right direction - on to the person of Christ and not the people around us.

Leaders do face many demands on their lives. Financial problems, people problems, work demands, difficult decisions, demanding supervisors, critical and dissatisfied followers, many things cause anxieties. Leadership can be a lonely job. Some times you feel it is a thankless job. Always in the firing line. Taking everyone's nonsense. Being disappointed by others. Difficult to please everyone. Criticised from within and without.

But…

The impact of a leader's discouragement on others can be devastating. Often people become the brunt of our worries and hassles. We take our insecurities and frustrations on family, colleagues and friends - causing unnecessary pain in the 'flock'. Too many people live with wounded spirits and under constant condemnation and find it difficult to enter a life of joy and grace because they are enslaved under a leader who saps true spiritual life.

We as shepherds are the Chief Shepherd's greatest concern - He knows what the small shepherds are going through - dealing with a set of challenges that often lead to discouragement, resentment and bitterness. So…cast it in the right direction - on to Him.

He has big shoulders.

Reflection

1. Can you name people who suffered because you could not handle your problems well, and you were casting in the wrong direction?

2. Can you name recent experiences in which you had to cast your cares upon the Lord, and you did not? What were the outcomes of those?

3. On a scale of 1 to 10, how reliant are you on the strength of the Lord, and how reliant would you want to be?

Reference
Reading & Author List

PART I

Chapter 1

1. Geoff Rutter, *Leadership and Management* - What the Bible Says,
2. Viscount Montgomery of *The Memoirs of Field Marshal Montgomery,* (Pen and Sword, November 2005)
3. J. Robert Clinton, *The Making of a Leader* (Navpress Publishing Group, October 1988)
4. Garry Wills, *Certain Trumpets: The Nature of Leadership* (A Touchstone Book), (Simon & Schuster Inc, May 1995)
5. Warren Bennis, *On Becoming A Leader* (Perseus Books Group; 1st edition, January 15, 1994)

Chapter 2

1. Abraham Zaleznik et...al, *Harvard Business Review* on Leadership (Harvard Business School Press September 1998)
2. Warren Bennis, *On Becoming A Leader* (Perseus Books Group; 1st edition, January 15, 1994)
3. Manfred Kets De Vries, *The Leadership Mystique* (New York, Prentice Hall, 2006)
4. Geoff Rutter, *Leadership and Management - What the Bible Says,*
5. Charles R. Swindoll, *Hand Me Another Brick,* Rev. and expanded Ed. (Nashville: Word Pub, c1998).

Chapter 4

1. Charles Gordon , *Successful Christian Leadership'* (manual)

Chapter 5

1. Rick Warren, *The Purpose Driven Life: What on earth I am I here for?* (Zondervan: Grand Rapids, Michigan, 2002)

2. Rick Warren, *The Purpose Driven Church: Growth without compromising your message and mission,* (Zondervan: Grand Rapids, Michigan, 1995)

Chapter 6

1. Geoff Rutter, *Leadership and Management* - What the Bible Says,

2. Fred Polak, *The Image of the Future.* (Oceana, 1961; Two Volumes.)

3. Joel A. Barker, *Paradigms: Business of Discovering the Future,* The Reprint edition (Collins; May 26, 1993)

Chapter 8

1. Geoff Rutter, *Leadership and Management - What the Bible Says,*

2. David Johnson and Jeff van Vonderen, *The Subtle Power of Spiritual Abuse* (Minneapolis, Minn:Bethany House, 2005)

Chapter 10

1. John Maxwell, *Developing the Leader within You,* (Nashville, Thomas Nelson, 1993)

2. John Maxwell, *Leadership 101: What every Leader needs to Know,* (Thomas Nelson, Nashville TN, 2002)

Chapter 11

1. Tim Elmore, *Mentoring: How to Invest your Life in Others* (Kingdom Pub. House 1995)

2. John Perry, *Christian Leadership*

PART II

Chapter 12

1. Ken Blanchard, *The Heart of a Leader* (Tulsa, Okla: Honor Books, 1994)

Chapter 13

1. Charles Gordon , *Successful Christian Leadership* (manual)

Chapter 14

1. George Barna, *Leaders on Leadership* (Ventura, Calif., USA: Regal Books, 1997)

2. Leighton Ford, *Helping Leaders Grow*

Chapter 16

1. Tim La Haye, *Spirit-Controlled Temperament,* Rev ed, (Wheaton, Ill.: Tyndale House Publishers; September 1993)

Chapter 18

1. Stephen Covey, *The Seven Habits of Highly Effective People: Personal Lessons in Personal Change,* (New York: Free Press, 2004)

2. Wilkinson, Bruce, *The Seven Laws of a Learner,* (Multinomah Press: Atlanta, Ga, 1992)

Chapter 19

1. Paul D. Stanley & Robert J. Clinton, *Connecting: The Mentoring Relationship you need to Succeed in Life,* (Colorado Springs, Colo: Nav press, 1992)

2. Leighton Ford, *Transforming leadership* (Downers Grove, Ill: Intervarsity Press, 1991)

Chapter 20

1. Kenneth Prior. *Perils of leadership: Overcoming personal battles,* (Downers grove, Ill.: Intervarsity press, 1990)

Chapter 23

1. Geoff Rutter, *'The loneliness of command'* article cited in the *'The Edge'* magazine 2000/1 edition.

2. Bishop Fulton J. Sheen quote

PART III

Chapter 24

1. James Emery White & William H. Willimon, *'Two leaders debate the value of transparency in ministry,* cited in the Leadership Journal 1998

Chapter 25

1. *The Youth Bible* (New Century Version, Booksite Africa and Struik Publishers)

Chapter 26

1. Anthony Laird, *'What I Wish I'd Known Before I Quit: Lessons from a Pastor who left too soon'*, http://www.leadershipjournal.net (November 8, 2000)

Chapter 28

1. Clive Douglas, *Property Management and Maintenance'* (Youth For Christ, YFC paper)

Chapter 29

1. Fred Smith, *'Conducting a Spiritual Audit'* http://www.leadershipjournal.net (Winter,1998)

2. Francois Fenelon, http://www.quotationsbook.com

Chapter 31

1. Oxford English Dictionary (Oxford University Press,2000)

PART IV

Chapter 32

1. *The Little & Ives Webster dictionary and home reference library: complete and unabridged.* International ed. (New York, J. J. Little & Ives Co. 1957)

2. New Testament Dictionary

3. Terry Virgo, *God's Amazing Grace,* (Orlando, Fla.: Christian Life Books; Lake Mary, FL:, 1993)

4. Chuck Pierce, Rebecca Wagner Sytsema, *When God Speaks* (Ventura, Calif.: Gospel Light, 2005)

Chapter 33

1. Henry Okullu, *Church and politics in East Africa.* (Nairobi, Kenya: Uzima Press, 1974)

2. Dietrich Bonhoeffer, *'Disillusioned with Your Church?,'* (Leadership Journal articles, Winter 98) p. 37

3. David Johnson and Jeff Van Vonderen, *The Subtle Power of Spiritual Abuse* (Bethany House Publishers, October 1991)

4. Geoff Rutter, *Leadership and Management* - What the Bible Says,

5. Louw Alberts

Chapter 34

1. George Barna, *Leaders on Leadership* (Ventura, Calif., USA: Regal Books, 1997)

2. Leighton Ford, *Helping Leaders Grow*

3. Stephen Covey, *The Seven Habits of Highly Effective People: Personal Lessons in Personal Change,* (New York: Free Press, 2004)

4. Rick Warren, *The Purpose Driven Church: Growth without compromising your message and mission,* (Zondervan: Grand Rapids, Michigan, 1995)

5. Wallace Erickson, *'Transition in Leadership' cited on Leaders on Leadership: Wisdom, Advice and Encouragement on the Art of Leading God's People* (Regal Books, May 1998)

Chapter 35

1. Life Application Bible
2. *The Little & Ives Webster dictionary and home reference library: complete and unabridged.* International ed. (New York, J. J. Little & Ives Co. 1957)
3. David Johnson and Jeff Van Vonderen, *The Subtle Power of Spiritual Abuse* (Bethany House Publishers, October 1991)

Chapter 36

1. Oxford English Dictionary (Oxford University Press, 2000)
2. George Sweeting, (notes from talk)
3. Stephen Covey et..al, *First things first every day : because where you're headed is more important than how fast you're going* (New York : Simon & Schuster, 1997)

Chapter 38

1. Ken Blanchard, *The Heart of a Leader* (Tulsa, Okla: Honor Books, 1994)
2. Frederick Herzberg, Bernard Mausner, *The Motivation to Work,* Reprint edition (Transaction Publishers; January 1, 1993)

Chapter 39

1. John Perry, *Effective Christian Leadership,* (Hodder & Stoughton, 1983)
2. Kenneth O. Gangel, *'What Leaders Do' cited on Leaders on Leadership: Wisdom, Advice and Encouragement on the Art of Leading God's People* (Regal Books, May 1998)
3. James MacGregor Burns, *Leadership* (New York: Harper & Row, 1979)

Chapter 41

1. Alan Loy McGinnis, *The Balanced Life: Achieving Success in Work & Love* (Augsburg Fortress Publishers, July 1997)
2. George Shinn, *Leadership Development* (McGraw-Hill/Glencoe January 1986)
3. James Dobson,
4. Samuel Johnson,

PART V

Chapter 42

1. John C. Maxwell, *The 21 Irrefutable Laws of Leadership* (Nashville: Thomas Nelson Publishers, September, 1998)

2. David L. Bradford and Allan R. Cohen, *Managing for Excellence; The Guide to Developing High Performance in Contemporary Organizations,* (John Wiley & Sons, 1984.)

3. Lovett H. Weems, *Church Leadership: Vision, Team, Culture and Integrity* (Abingdon Press September 1993)

4. Max DePree, *Leadership Jazz* Reprint edition (Dell, September, 1993)

5. Max DePree *Leadership Is an Art* Reprint edition (Currency, May, 2004)

Chapter 43

1. John C. Maxwell, *The 21 Irrefutable Laws of Leadership* (Nashville: Thomas Nelson Publishers, September, 1998)

2. Wallace Erickson, *'Transition in Leadership'* cited on *Leaders on Leadership: Wisdom, Advice and Encouragement on the Art of Leading God's People* (Regal Books, May 1998)

3. Peter Drucker,

Chapter 44

1. Hans Finzel, *'Creating the Right Leadership Culture'* cited on *Leaders on Leadership: Wisdom, Advice and Encouragement on the Art of Leading God's People* (Regal Books, May 1998)

2. *The Little & Ives Webster dictionary and home reference library: complete and unabridged.* International ed. (New York, J. J. Little & Ives Co. 1957)

3. Lovett H. Weems, *Church Leadership: Vision, Team, Culture and Integrity* (Abingdon Press September 1993)

Chapter 45

1. Farmers Digest,

2. Francis Schaeffer,

3. Elbert Hubbard,

4. Neville Riddick

Chapter 46

1. Kenneth H. Blanchard, William Oncken Jr., Hal Burrows, *The One Minute Manager Meets the Monkey* Reprint edition (William Morrow & Company, January 1991)

2. Geoff Rutter, *Leadership and Management - What the Bible Says,*

3. Stephen Covey et..al, *First things first every day : because where you're headed is more important than how fast you're going* (New York : Simon & Schuster, 1997)

Chapter 47

1. Geoff Rutter, *Leadership and Management - What the Bible Says,*

2. Charles R. Swindoll, *Hand me another Brick,* (Nashville, Thomas Nelson, 1990)

Chapter 48

1. Ronald S. Combs *Preacher's Magazine* (Beacon Hill Press: Kansas, 1978)

Chapter 49

1. Peter C. Wagner, *Discover Your Spiritual Gifts* Exp & Updated edition (Regal Books, March 2005)

2. John McArthur

3. Vineyard Ministries International,

4. Ravi Zacharias International Ministries

Chapter 51

1. Kenneth Prior. Perils of leadership: *Overcoming personal battles,* (Downers grove, Ill.: Intervarsity press, 1990)

2. Arlo Walker, *'Are Pastors Abused'* cited on ChristianityToday.com

Chapter 52

1. Ken Blanchard, Bill Hybels *Leadership by the Book: Tools to Transform your Workplace* (Colorado Springs:Co, Waterbrook Press, 1999)

Chapter 53

1. Ken Blanchard, Bill Hybels *Leadership by the Book: Tools to Transform your Workplace* (Colorado Springs:Co, Waterbrook Press, 1999

2. Charles R. Swindoll, cited on *A Deeper Faith magazine* http://www.gra-son.org

3. Patrick M. Morley, *The Man in the Mirror: Solving the 24 problems Men Face* (Grand Rapids, Michigan; Zondervan, 1997)

Chapter 54

1. John C. Maxwell, *The 21 Irrefutable Laws of Leadership* (Nashville: Thomas Nelson Publishers, September, 1998)

2. Oxford English Dictionary (Oxford University Press, 2000)

3. Doug Murren, *Leader Shift: How to Avoid Paradigm Shock* (Kingdom

Publishing,September 1999)

4. Doug Murren, *Leadershift: How to Lead Your Church into the 21st Century by Managing Change* (Regal Books, September 1993)

5. Martin E. Seligman, *Learned Optimism: How to Change Your Mind and Your Life* Reissue edition (Free Press, March, 1998)

6. Denis Waitley, *The Winner's Edge*, Reissue edition (Berkley, November, 1986)

Chapter 55

1. Geoff Rutter, *Leadership and Management - What the Bible Says,*

2. Paul, Chaffee, *Accountable Leadership:A resource Guide for sustaining legal, financial and ethical integrity in today's congregations,* (California;Jossey-Bass Publishers, 1997)

3. Lee Iacocca with William Novak, *Iacocca: An Autobiography* New York:Bantam Books, 1984)

PART VI

Chapter 56

1. Charles R. Swindoll, *Strengthening your Grip,* (Nashville; Word Publishers, 1998)

2. Myron Bush, *Managing to be the Best: A Personal Approach,* (Wheaton, Ill: Victor Books, 1989)

3. Alan Loy McGinnis, *The Balanced Life: Achieving Success in Work & Love* (Augsburg Fortress Publishers, July 1997)

4. Patty Marler, Jan Bailey Mattia, *Time Management Made Easy,* (Lincolnwood, ill;VGM Career Horizons, 1998)

5. Gordon MacDonald, *Restoring Your Spiritual Passion,* (Nashville: Oliver-Nelson Books, 1986)

6. Edwin C. Bliss, *Getting Things Done* (Scribner, August, 1976)

7. Geoffrey Moss, *Survival Skills for New Managers,* (CCH Australia Limited, 1992)

Chapter 57

1. Tom Marshall, *Understanding Leadership,* (Baker Books,May 2003)

Chapter 58

1. David L. Hocking, *Be a Leader People Follow,* (Glendale, Calif; Regal Books, 1979)

Chapter 59

1. Kenneth A. Erickson, *Christian Time Management,* (St. Louis,MO; Concordia Publishing House, 1985)

2. Edwin C. Bliss, *Getting Things Done* (Scribner,August, 1976)

3. Verne Becker,cited in *'Today's Christian Woman,'*1981 edition

Chapter 60

1. Ken Blanchard, Bill Hybels *Leadership by the Book: Tools to Transform your Workplace*(Colorado Springs:Co, Waterbrook Press, 1999)

2. Tom Marshall, *Understanding Leadership,* (Baker Books,May 2003)

Chapter 61

1. Ibid.

Chapter 63

1. Kairos International, *Leadership Beyond Management*

2. Raymond L. Hilgert; James L. Truesdell; Philip H. Lochhaas, *Christian Ethics in the Workplace* (Concordia Publishing House, November 2001)

PART VII

Chapter 64

1. Louis V. Gerstner Jr., *Who Says Elephants Can't Dance? Inside IBM's Historic Turnaround* (Collins, November, 2002)

2. Tom Marshall, *Understanding Leadership,* (Baker Books,May 2003)

Chapter 66

1. Howard G. Hendricks, *Color Outside the Lines* (W Publishing Group, September, 2002)

2. Eugene Peterson

3. John W. Garner

4. Peter Drucker

Chapter 67

1. Nancy Hunter Denney, James Malinchak et..al *Let Your Leadership Speak: How to Lead and Be Heard* (Central Plains Book Publishing, April 2002)

2. Dale Carnegie

3. Winston Churchill

Chapter 68

1. Randy Haveson

2. Kairos International

Chapter 69

1. Nancy Hunter Denney, James Malinchak et..al *Let Your Leadership Speak: How to Lead and Be Heard* (Central Plains Book Publishing, April 2002)

PART VIII

Chapter 70

1. Patty Marler, Jan Bailey Mattia, *Time Management Made Easy,* (Lincolnwood, ill; VGM Career Horizons, 1998)

2. Johan Wolfgang von Goethe

3. Thomas Fuller

Chapter 72

1. Robert Welch

Chapter 73

1. Edwin C. Bliss, *Getting Things Done* (Scribner, August, 1976)

2. Anitra Rasmussen

3. Oscar Wilde

Chapter 74

1. Ted Carr, *Former National Director of Youth For Christ YFC, South Africa*

Chapter 76

1. Manfred Kets De Vries, *The Leadership Mystique* (New York, Prentice Hall, 2006)

Chapter 77

1. Howard G. Hendricks, *Color Outside the Lines* (W Publishing Group, September, 2002)

2. Rodney Thorne

3. Byrd Baggett

Chapter 78

1. Louis V. Gerstner Jr., *Who Says Elephants Can't Dance? Inside IBM's Historic Turnaround* (Collins, November, 2002)

2. John Rae, Theo Jansen, *'Preparing for Implementing and Manging a*

Superior Client Care Culture in your Company' Manual

Chapter 79

1. C. S. Lewis, *Mere Christianity* (HarperSanFrancisco; Harper edition ,February, 2001)

Chapter 80

1. Kairos International, *Leadership Beyond Management*
2. Peter Drucker

PART IX

Chapter 81

1. John R. W. Stott, *Decisive Issues Facing Christians Today,* (Fleming H Revell Co, February 1996)

Chapter 83

1. The Poetry of Robert Frost: The Collected Poems, Complete and Unabridged (Henry Holt and Co.; 1st Owl edition, November, 1969)
2. Peter Drucker

Chapter 84

1. John R. W. Stott, *Decisive Issues Facing Christians Today,* (Fleming H Revell Co, February 1996)

Chapter 85

1. Manfred Kets De Vries, *The Leadership Mystique* (New York, Prentice Hall, 2006)
2. Prosci's *ADKAR Model,* http://www.change-management.com/Tutorial-ADKAR-series-2.htm

Chapter 87

1. Aubrey Malphurs, *The Dynamics of Church Leadership, Ministry Dynamics for a New Century,* (Baker Books, October 1999)
2. Tom Marshall, *Understanding Leadership,* (Baker Books, May 2003)
3. Robert A. Cook, cited on http://www.brainyquote.com/quotes/authors/r/robert_a_cook.
4. Barry Gibbons,
5. Jack W. Hayford,

Chapter 88

1. Oxford English Dictionary (Oxford University Press, 2000)
2. Mark Caine, http://www.quotationsbook.com

Chapter 89

1. Robert Half, Finding, *Hiring, and Keeping the Best Employees;* 1 edition (John Wiley & Sons, October, 1993)

PART X

Chapter 90

1. Aristotle, http://www.quotationsbook.com
2. Bill Hybels, *Courageous Leadership* (Nairobi, Kenya: Evangel Pub. House, 2004)
3. Ibid.

Chapter 91

1. Stephen Covey, *The Seven Habits of Highly Effective People: Personal Lessons in Personal Change,* (New York: Free Press, 2004)
2. Johan Wolfgang von Goethe
3. Edwin Markham, cited on http://www.brainyquote.com

Chapter 92

1. Lindie Haarhof, *Winning Edge Developments*

Chapter 93

1. Elinor Smith, *American aviator,*

Chapter 94

1. John C. Maxwell, *The Maxwell Leadership Bible Developing Leaders From The Word Of God* (Nelson Bibles, March, 2002)

Chapter 95

1. *The Economist*
2. Michael Schrage,
3. David Wraight, *President YFCI*

Chapter 97

1. John C. Maxwell, *The 21 Irrefutable Laws of Leadership* (Nashville: Thomas Nelson Publishers, September, 1998)
2. Wallace Erickson, *'Transition in Leadership'* cited on *Leaders on*

Leadership: Wisdom, Advice and Encouragement on the Art of Leading God's People (Regal Books, May 1998)

Chapter 98

1. Oxford English Dictionary (Oxford University Press, 2000)

Chapter 99

1. Eugene H. Peterson, *The Message: the Bible in Contemporary Language,* Pocket edition (Navpress Publishing Group, July 2004)

2. David Wraight, *President YFCI*

YFCI'S PHILOSOPHY AND THEOLOGY OF LEADERSHIP

Youth for Christ (YFC) has a rich history of over 60 years of reaching young people with the Gospel of Jesus Christ. Millions of young people have made commitments to Christ during this 60-year history, but as we look to the future we have a growing sense that God is directing us to re-align our focus; to not just seek conversions to Christ, but to grow disciples and allow these disciples to lead YFC into the future.

Over the past five years, God has taken YFC through a process of soul-searching and spiritual renewal, involving an extensive period of worldwide prayer, consultancy, restructure and planning.

This has culminated in a redirection of the primary focus of our ministry. God has clearly directed YFC to move from making converts to making disciples; to not only reach young people but to continue to be engaged in the process of nurturing and discipling these young people; to grow disciples who will be committed, vibrant and on fire for God and will be agents of change in the church and in the world.

Jesus commanded us to 'go and make disciples of all nations' (Matt 28:19). In this new era of ministry for YFC, we believe God has called us specifically to 'make disciples' who are 'disciple makers'.

When young people are given the freedom to lead, amazing fruit is produced. Young people have boundless energy. Their healthy naiveté constantly generates courageous and creative initiatives, and their connectedness to the youth community allows them to be relevant and effective in their mission to them.

By involving young people at the most strategic levels of ministry in YFC worldwide, we will continue to remain at the cutting edge of youth ministries. We need to empower younger leaders and allow them to lead the ministry, harnessing their potential to reach and disciple young people.

The development of a new generation of leaders world wide therefore, is fundamental to the success of our global strategic mission. This new generation of leaders are the key to our mission accomplishment. In all the consultations we have done with our staff and others in Christian ministry, the issue of Leadership Development has risen to the top as the most important investment and priority.

We believe in and are committed to the primary goals of Biblical leadership which are:

- To Make Disciples, (Matt 28:18-20)
- To Care for and nurture the people of God, (1 Peter 5:2-3)
- To Equip God's people for service with a view toward maturity, (Eph. 4:11-13
- To Reproduce leaders, (II Tim. 2:2)

To have the 'right' leaders we need to develop the 'right' training, guided and informed by a leadership profile that paints a clear picture of what the end product should look like. This has led us to develop a comprehensive profile of a leader. This profile provides a framework for us to design and develop materials and models for leadership development and it also gives us a point of reference to evaluate our effectiveness.

This book on leadership, is one of the tools that has been provided to get us going on the road of leadership development. Our goal is to help raise a new generation of leaders within YFC, and the Christian community, whose lives will reflect godly character and a burning passion for making disciples who lead by, devotion to prayer and the Word of God, passion for sharing the love of Christ, their godliness in lifestyle and commitment to social involvement.

The Profile of a leader also give us a point of reference to evaluate our leadership development programs in YFC and to plan new approaches to ministry to provide the infrastructure that will enable us to effectively nurture and empower young people to be world-changing disciples of Jesus.

Character

Has a Heart for God
- Passionate desire to be in God's presence, through prayer and communion with Him. (Psalm 42:1; Phil 3:7-10)
- Has a ministry and personal life under-girded by prayer and the Word of God. (Acts 2:42; 1 Thess 5:17; Psalm 1:1-3; Josh 1:8)
- Pursues personal holiness and obedience to the Scripture. (Lev 11:44-45; 1Cor 1:2; Eph 1:4; Heb 12:14; 1 Pet 1:15-16)
- Relies on God to minister through them. (Phil 4:13; John 15:4, 5; Acts

17:28; Psalm 121)

- Worships God with His people. (Heb 10:25; Gal 5:13)

Has a clear calling and vision from God

- Has a clear calling from God to serve Him and His people. (Jer 1:5; John 20:21; Rom 1:1, 8:28-30; 1 Pet 2:9-10)
- Has a vision of what God wants them to do. (Gen 45:5-7; Jer 26:12; Acts 26:19-23)

Has a heart for young People

- Prays with and intercedes for young people consistently. (Eph 1:16; Eph 6:18; Col 4:2-4)
- Demonstrates an active love for young people. (1 Cor 4:17; Phil 4:1; 2 John 1:1)
- Acts compassionately toward those who are hurting. (1 Kings 3:26; Luke 10:30-37; Phil 2:1-4)
- Enjoys being with young people and relates to them effectively. (Matt 5:13-15; 1Thess 1:5)
- Committed to appropriate relationships with youth.

Is maturing personally

- Seeks the mind of Christ and His Kingdom perspective. (Rom 8:29; 1 Cor 2:15,16)
- Demonstrates integrity and speaks the truth. (1 Tim 2:1-2, 4:12, 6:11; Psalm 78:72, 22:11)
- Know their gifts, personality, emotional strengths and weaknesses. (Psalm 139:23; James 1:23-24; 2 Cor 12:9-10; Rom 12:5-13; Eph 4:11-13)

Family life for married staff

Maintains a healthy relationship

- Models biblical boundaries in marriage. (Eph 5:22-6:4; Heb 13:4-5; Col 3:18-21; 1 Thess 4:3-8)
- Has a growing and positive vibrant relationship with spouse. (Rom 12:10; Eph 5:1-2)
- Places a non-negotiable value on time spent with spouse. (Gen 2:24; Matt 19:5-6; Rom 12:10; 1Cor 7:3-4)
- Encourages and nurtures intimacy with God with spouse. (Josh 24:15; Eph 5:31; Heb 10:24)

Maintains healthy family relationships

- Maintains a healthy balance between family and ministry. (1 Tim 3:12; 1 Tim 5:8)
- Applies good parenting skills. (Prov 22:6; 1Tim 3:12)
- Encourages and nurtures intimacy with God within family. (Josh 24:15, Eph

5:31, Heb 10:24)

Family life for single staff

Maintains healthy relationships

- Models biblical boundaries in relationships. (Rom 13:13; 1 Cor 6:18-20; 1 Thess 4:3-8)
- Is totally committed to positive and loving relationship with family members and acquaintances. (Rom 12:10; Eph 5:1-2; 1 Peter 4:9)
- Maintains a healthy and positive image of who they are in Christ and are willing to accept God's will concerning their marital status. (Matt 6:25-33; Col 2:9-10; 1 Thess 5:18; 1 Peter 2:9)
- Encourages and nurtures intimacy with God with dates and or acquaintances. (Josh 24:15; Eph 5:31; Heb 10:24)

Maintains healthy family relationships

- Maintains a healthy balance between family and personal life and ministry. (1Tim 3:12; 1Tim 5:8)
- Encourages and nurtures intimacy with God within family. (Josh 24:15; Eph 5:31; Heb 10:24)

Leadership

Leads like Jesus

- Articulates and demonstrates Christ-like leadership. (Luke 9:46-48, 22:24-30; John 15:13-15; 2 Cor 4:5; 1 Peter 5:2-4)
- Has a servant attitude toward others. (Matt 20:26, 23:11-12; John 13:1-17; 1 Peter 4:10)
- Practices team ministry. (Ex 18:13-26; Matt 10:2-4; Luke 6:12-16; Acts 6:1-6)
- Develops leaders and disciples. (Ex 35:34; Psalm 78:5-7; Matt 28:19,20; 2 Tim 2:2)
- Enables and develops followers. (2 Kings 2:1-15; Acts 20:17-21; 1 Thess 1:4-2:9)
- Develops strategy for ministry. (1 Chron 28:11-19; Psalm 20:4; Prov 15:22, 16:9, 20:18)
- Communicates vision and purpose effectively. (Prov 29:18; Acts 26:2-23; 2 Cor 5:6-10; Col 2:2-5; 2 Tim 3:10-17)

Manages themselves and others effectively

- Can recruit, build and supervise a team. (Ex 18:13-26; Matt 10:2-4; Luke 6:12-16; Acts 6:1-6)
- Can manage self and ministry priorities well. (Luke 12:48; Matt 25:14-29)
- Can strategize, plan, organize, evaluate and report. (1 Chron 28:11-19; Psalm 20:4; Prov 15:22, 16:9, 20:18; Luke 14:28-33)

- Can manage budget, raise funds, and control them responsibly. (Gen 41:46-57; 1 Kings 6-7; Ezra 1:5-11; Luke 12:32-48,16:1-13; 1 Cor 4:1-4, 1 Pet 4:10)

Skillfully leads people

- Understands their own leadership style, and can adapt it to a team's needs. (Num 27:15-23; Judges 4:4-16; Acts 6:1-6; 1 Peter 5:2-4)
- Can engage conflict constructively, and lead teams in reconciliation. (Ex 18:13-26; Acts 6:1-6; Matt 5:9, 18:15-20; 2 Cor 5:18-21; Eph 4:3; James 3:18)
- Uses appropriate strategies for problem solving and decision making. (1 Kings 3:16-28; Acts 6:1-4; Gal 6:1-10)
- Communicates well throughout the organization. (Rom 1:7; 1 Cor 1:2; Gal 1:2; James 1:1; 1 Peter 1:1; Rev 1:4)
- Continually seeks input and feedback. (2 Chron 32:1-8; Prov 15:22, 27:9; Esther 6:6-9; Matt 16:13-20)

Evangelism

Is passionate and sensitive about evangelism

- Seeks opportunities for evangelism. (Rom 1:15, 15:20; Acts 17:2-34; Col 4:2-4)
- Can train and mobilize others for evangelism. (Matt 28:19-20; Luke 9:1-6; 2 Tim 2:2)
- Uses creative approaches for evangelism. (Mark 2:1-12)

Is aware of the world and sees trends in today's generation

- Shows awareness of the community and culture around them and assesses young people's needs. (Matt 10:22; Luke 6:22; Phil 2:15; Hebrews 11; 1 Cor 8:1-13)
- Understands trends in youth cultures, and responds accordingly. (1 Chron 12:32; Acts 17:16-34)
- Is aware of the tensions between the Gospel and culture. (Matt 10:22; Luke 6:22; Phil 2:15; Hebrews 11; 1 Cor 8:1-13)
- Is aware of what God is doing through His people. (Acts 15:2-4; Psalm 46:6-11)
- Has compassion for people in other countries. (Luke 10:25-37; Acts 11:27-30; Col 3:12)
- Participates in local and global missions. (Mark 16:15; Acts 1:8, 8:25, 40; Rom 15:20)

Kingdom Seeking

Has a heart for the growth of the Body of Christ

- Committed to equipping and mobilizing God's people for service. (Eph 4:11-13)